PHP 8 Basics

For Programming and Web Development

Gunnard Engebreth
Satej Kumar Sahu

Apress®

PHP 8 Basics: For Programming and Web Development

Gunnard Engebreth
Madison, WI, USA

Satej Kumar Sahu
Bangalore, India

ISBN-13 (pbk): 978-1-4842-8081-2
https://doi.org/10.1007/978-1-4842-8082-9

ISBN-13 (electronic): 978-1-4842-8082-9

Managing Director, Apress Media LLC: Welmoed Spahr
Acquisitions Editor: Steve Anglin
Development Editor: James Markham
Coordinating Editor: Mark Powers
Copy Editor: Mary Behr

Cover designed by eStudioCalamar

Cover image by Hugol Halpingston on Unsplash (www.unsplash.com)

Distributed to the book trade worldwide by Apress Media, LLC, 1 New York Plaza, New York, NY 10004, U.S.A. Phone 1-800-SPRINGER, fax (201) 348-4505, e-mail orders-ny@springer-sbm.com, or visit www.springeronline.com. Apress Media, LLC is a California LLC and the sole member (owner) is Springer Science + Business Media Finance Inc (SSBM Finance Inc). SSBM Finance Inc is a **Delaware** corporation.

For information on translations, please e-mail booktranslations@springernature.com; for reprint, paperback, or audio rights, please e-mail bookpermissions@springernature.com.

Apress titles may be purchased in bulk for academic, corporate, or promotional use. eBook versions and licenses are also available for most titles. For more information, reference our Print and eBook Bulk Sales web page at www.apress.com/bulk-sales.

Any source code or other supplementary material referenced by the author in this book is available to readers on GitHub (https://github.com/Apress). For more detailed information, please visit www.apress.com/source-code.

Printed on acid-free paper

*This book is dedicated to my wife Erica
and to my boys Trip and Wyatt.
Also, you the reader.
Thank you!*

*Jesus looked at them and said,
"With man this is impossible,
but with God all things are possible."*
—Matthew 19:26!

Table of Contents

About the Authors

Gunnard Engebreth began coding at the age of 11 through a "Learning BASIC" book given to him by his father. Technology was changing fast, and Gunnard rode the wave from 1200 to 56k baud modems. Logging into BBSs, Prodigy, CompuServe, Delphi, and IRC, he could see the world changing and he wanted to be a part of it. He soon got involved in the ANSI/demo scene, making several application generators for many groups in the 1990s. Visual Basic was his next language of choice, allowing him to develop "tools" for online systems such as AOL. This introduced many aspects of development, security, and user interfaces while they were still in their infancy. Once the World Wide Web arrived via Mindspring in Atlanta, Georgia, Gunnard quickly joined in the race for the Web. Learning HTML, PERL, and Linux (Slackware at the time), he began to build his skill set, which led to a full-time systems administrator position at the age of 20 (2000) at Activegrams/Silverpop. Gunnard has moved around the IT industry from SAN/NAS storage at IBM to custom WordPress sites for marketing companies, but one thing has stayed the same: his passion for learning and problem solving. Gunnard also DJs drum and bass as Section31, plays drums, and bakes bread (`www.gunnard.org`).

Satej Kumar Sahu works in the role of Senior Software Data Architect at Boeing. He is passionate about technology, people, and nature. He believes that through technology and conscientious decision making, each of us has the power to make this world a better place. In his free time, he can be found reading books, playing basketball, and having fun with friends and family.

About the Contributor

 **Massimo Nardone** has more than 26 years of experience in security, web/mobile development, and cloud and IT architecture. His true IT passions are security and Android. He has been programming and teaching how to program with Android, Perl, PHP, Java, VB, Python, C/C++, and MySQL for more than 25 years. He holds a Master of Science degree in Computing Science from the University of Salerno, Italy. He has worked as a Chief Information Security Office (CISO), software engineer, chief security architect, security executive, OT/IoT/IIoT Security Leader, and architect for many years.

Acknowledgments

I would like to dedicate this book to my parents for always believing in and having patience with me while I pursued my interest in technology, and gave me the freedom to explore and try different things. Also, thanks to my sister Lipsa for always being beside me whenever I needed her. I would like to thank all my teachers for being with me during my journey, Runish for the foundational mentoring support at the start of my career, Mindfire Solutions for my first career opportunity, and to all with whom I had an opportunity to interact and learn from. Last but not least I would like to thank Mark for the awesome opportunity to write my first book and the wonderful team at Apress for all their support without whom this book would not have been possible.

Introduction

Developing web pages and applications is still, after many years, one of the most fascinating endeavors for developers. The idea of taking a simple idea and developing it, seeing it coming alive and imagining the experience the user will have is something very magical.

The experience of programming as web developer should, of course, also be easy, user-friendly, and flexible—all characteristics of the programming language this book is all about: PHP version 8.

The first version of PHP was created by Rasmus Lerdorf in 1994 and he mainly used it on his home page to keep track of who was looking at his online resume. In 1995, the first public version was published as the Personal Home Page Tools.

In the beginning, PHP was just a simple programming language with a very easy parser engine that only understood a small number of utilities and macros.

PHP usage grown. In 1996, about 15,000 web sites were developed with PHP; by 1997, it was up to 50,000. In 1999, about 1 million web sites were developed with PHP. At the time of writing, 78 million of web sites have been developed with PHP to give you a perspective of how popular this programming language has become. Why?

Simple. Because after many years it is still easy to use, user-friendly, and clearly organized. This helps would-be programmers easily understand and run PHP commands and functions.

We want to help PHP beginners and would-be developers explore the new features added to this version 8 and see how easy, flexible, and powerful it can be to develop new web sites and applications.

You will find all the basic information about how to install and configure PHP version 8.

All basic PHP concepts like data types, functions, regular expressions, form handling and verification, sessions, cookies, and filters are introduced and demonstrated with many examples.

We also introduce the basic information of object-oriented programming and its classes and objects.

This book also provides some simple examples about how to use PHP version 8 with one of the most powerful and used databases for developers, MySQL. You learn how to develop an entire web application using PHP version 8 and MySQL.

You also learn about PHP frameworks and why they are so important to use. This book focuses on just two of the many PHP frameworks available, Symfony and Laravel, and the development of web applications following the model–view–controller architectural pattern.

Who This Book Is For

The book assumes you have some web development and DB handling knowledge. The book is written mainly for the beginning web developer who wants to learn how to use PHP version 8 and how it can be used with MySQL and PHP frameworks like laravel and Symfony. It also assumes you have some knowledge of programing language frameworks and how and when you should use them with PHP.

Prerequisites

The examples in this book were built with PHP version 8. We also used MySQL for Ubuntu Linux version 22.04 DEB Bundle. As a testing tool, we used the latest Postman API client version available on the Web, but you are free to use any testing tool you feel comfortable with. Finally, we introduced and utilized two different PHP Frameworks named Laravel and Symfony, which will be needed for the examples of this book.

Downloading the Code

The source code for the examples in this book is available at `www.github.com/apress/php8-basics`.

CHAPTER 1

Getting Started

PHP is the de facto programming language used to serve billions ("BILL" not "MILL") a month. PHP has grown from a hodge-podge collection of scripts that could be used to stitch together a functional website into the backbone of several billion-dollar companies influencing how industry works across the globe. Yes, there are other languages out there that do many things, but you are not reading this book to understand them! You chose to step into the world of PHP and join the network of developers who focus on solutions, community, and the advancement of PHP. This chapter of the book will cover the why, when, and how of using the PHP programming language. It will also introduce some programming development environments and describe how to install Docker, which is an open platform for developing, shipping, and running applications.

Why Use PHP?

FACT: PHP runs the Web. This is a bold statement but just look at these numbers:

- Facebook: 25.7 billion monthly estimated visits

- Wikipedia: 15 billion monthly estimated visits

- Yahoo: 4.8 billion monthly estimated visits

- Flickr: 65.44 million monthly estimated visits

- Tumblr: 328.9 million monthly estimated visits

© Gunnard Engebreth, Satej Kumar Sahu 2023
G. Engebreth and S. K. Sahu, *PHP 8 Basics*, https://doi.org/10.1007/978-1-4842-8082-9_1

Any one of those sites above pull impressive numbers, but when combined, they are pretty hefty statistics. Even if you have a loyalty to another programming language, you can't deny the use of PHP as a workhorse in these sites. While we can see that large corporations have come to trust the language, what about average users like you and me? Over 39.5% of all websites on the Internet are run on WordPress. Let that sink in for a minute. Almost 40% of all websites are served up on a CMS (open source, no less) that is developed in PHP.

PHP is exploding yearly in terms of demand. A quick check on any job search website will give you thousands of results.

PHP is continuously growing, with scheduled releases and a thriving community of developers maintaining technological relevance.

PHP is the most exciting AND the most practical programming language you can get started with today.

Admittedly, we may have our biases.

Using PHP

PHP is mainly used by developers in two ways. One method is to organize and deliver data from a data source (i.e., a MySQL database) to a webpage. Think of Facebook or Twitter. The content that you see on these sites is stored somewhere in a database and needs to be retrieved and then parsed or organized, ultimately leading to a front-end display to the user. Your cousin's baby pictures with 40 likes must be gathered, the likes must be collected and names attributed to them, and then they are ready to pop up on your timeline. Depending on the infrastructure, this data can be stored in one location or multiple places, tied together with unique identifiers. We may be getting ahead of ourselves here, but we are trying to convey the fact that the information you see on webpages is cultivated by PHP from information stored in databases. PHP is the toolbox you will use to build these powerful applications.

We mentioned that there are two main ways to use PHP. The other way is on the command line. There are usually several scripting languages on a server that can be used to perform all sorts of tasks. Bash, Python, and Perl come to mind, but PHP can be used in the same way. If you have not already, go to the GitHub repo linked from this book's `apress.com` product page and look at the Chapter 1 link. From here, you will set up the development environment in order to look at and run these PHP scripts.

Let's get the development environment spun up so you can see PHP in action.

PHP is a server-side scripting language and therefore needs a server with the appropriate settings and resources to run. While PHP comes natively installed on many operating systems, it can be installed or upgraded on its own. Examples of other server-side languages are Python, Ruby, and Perl. The opposite of this is client-side languages. They are processed in the browser and are based on JavaScript. Examples of client-side languages are Vue.js, jQuery, and Node.js.

Why PHP, Ngnix, and MySQL?

Let us introduce you to your new best friends, at least in terms of your daily exposure to them. As a developer, you will need to work with each of these new friends intimately. PHP (as we have discussed) is the language in which we will be writing our scripts. Nginx is the web server, which allows for web pages to be served when a user accesses specific URLs on a server. When you go to `gunnard.org`, for example, the webserver at the hosting site looks at the URL (`www.gunnard.org`) and checks to see if there are any associated www settings (in Nginx) for this website. If there are, the software (Nginx) looks for the document root setting and directs the user to that location. Once there, the first thing the server will look at, unless otherwise specified, is an `index.html` or `index.php` page. The `index.html/php` paradigm is fairly standard across the board and serves as a failsafe to protect directories from being viewed across the Web. For example, if you have an `assets/` directory with private information that is publicly accessible, say `gunnard.org/assets`, but there is no `index.html`, this will be viewable to anyone, and they will see a list of files in that directory. If a blank `index.html` is placed there, the file will be shown instead. Within Nginx you can set the priority and order in which Nginx looks for these default files. When using PHP, it is necessary to specify that Nginx looks for `index.php` over `index.html`, for example.

In order to use your development environment, you need a tool called Docker. Docker provides your computer (the host machine) with the ability to masquerade as a web server, in your example, without creating a virtual machine separate from your host environment. This might sound like the exact thing you WANT to do, which it is, but Docker goes about it in a slightly different way that is more robust, easier to manage, and less invasive than your typical virtual machine. Think of Docker as software that allows for a container to dress up like a specific type of computer or server. This container is separate from your host system but also uses the resources (directories, CPU, memory) of your host without actually changing or creating a new machine. The inner workings of Docker vs. virtual machines is outside of the scope of this book and frankly could take an entire book to explain it much better than we just did. The bottom line is that with Docker, we control and can use the beneficial parts of a web server without having to create, install, and maintain a real or virtual server. Plus, as of printing, this is what 99% of development shops use; this is very industry standard.

Installing Docker

Let's get Docker installed on your operating system of choice. Here's how to do it.

Windows

Go to https://docs.docker.com/docker-for-windows/install/ and click the "Docker Desktop for Windows" button to download Docker, as shown in Figure 1-1.

Figure 1-1. *The Docker Desktop for Windows download button*

1. Double-click Docker Desktop Installer.exe to run the installer.

2. When prompted, ensure the Enable Hyper-V Windows Features. If you have previously configured WSL and are comfortable with it, then make sure the "Install required Windows components for WSL 2" option is selected on the Configuration page.

3. Follow the instructions in the installation wizard to authorize the installer and proceed with the install.

4. When the installation is successful, click Close to complete the installation process.

5. If your admin account is different to your user account, you must add the user to the docker-users group. Run Computer Management as an

administrator and navigate to Local Users and
Groups ➤ Groups ➤ docker-users. Right-click to
add the user to the group. Log out and log back in
for the changes to take effect.

Docker Desktop does not start automatically after installation. To
start Docker Desktop, search for Docker, and select Docker Desktop in the
search results. When the whale icon in the status bar stays steady, Docker
Desktop is up, running, and accessible from any terminal window.

Mac OS

Go to `https://docs.docker.com/docker-for-mac/install/,` shown in
Figure 1-2.

Figure 1-2. *Download options for Docker for Mac*

Double-click `Docker.dmg` to open the installer and then drag the
Docker icon to the `Applications` folder, as shown in Figure 1-3.

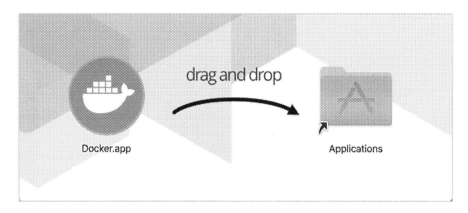

Figure 1-3. *Moving the Docker application to the Applications folder*

Double-click Docker.app in the Applications folder to start Docker.
(In Figure 1-4, the Applications folder is in grid view mode.)

Figure 1-4. *Docker Applications folder*

The Docker menu in the top status bar indicates that Docker Desktop
is running and accessible from a terminal.

Linux

Go to https://docs.docker.com/engine/install/. Here you will find
links to instructions on how to install Docker on several popular Linux

distributions. If you are using Debian/Ubuntu, you can follow these
instructions (https://docs.docker.com/engine/install/ubuntu/):

    1)   Ensure that any older installation is removed from
        the system.

```
<code>
 sudo apt-get remove docker docker-engine docker.io
 containerd runc
</code>
```

    2)   Update the apt package index and install packages
        to allow apt to use a repository over HTTPS.

```
<code>
 sudo apt-get update
 sudo apt-get install \
    apt-transport-https \
    ca-certificates \
    curl \
    gnupg \
    lsb-release
</code>
```

    3)   Add Docker's official GPG key.

```
<code>
curl -fsSL https://download.docker.com/linux/ubuntu/gpg | sudo
gpg --dearmor -o /usr/share/keyrings/docker-archive-keyring.gpg
</code>
```

    4)   Use the following command to set up the stable
        repository. To add the nightly or test repository,
        add the word nightly or test (or both) after the
        word stable.

```
<code>
echo \
  "deb [arch=amd64 signed-by=/usr/share/keyrings/docker-archive-
  keyring.gpg] https://download.docker.com/linux/ubuntu \
  $(lsb_release -cs) stable" | sudo tee /etc/apt/sources.
  list.d/docker.list > /dev/null
</code>
```

    5)   Update the apt package index and install the latest
         version of Docker Engine and container.

```
<code>
sudo apt-get update
sudo apt-get install docker-ce docker-ce-cli containerd.io
</code>
```

If you have any difficulties or need to install a specific version of Docker for your system, please visit https://docs.docker.com/engine/ install/ where they cover many more options and configurations than is possible in the scope of this section.

Once Docker is installed, you will need to install docker-compose. Compose is a tool for defining and running multi-container Docker applications. Compose allows you to define an application within the confines of a YAML (Yet Another Markup Language) file. This allows you to spin up all of the defined services for your Docker container with a single command. This is often used within development teams to ensure version control and maintain use of third-party applications. Other features of Compose are

- Multiple isolated environments on a single host

- Preserving volume data when containers are created

- Only recreating containers that have changed

- Variables and moving a composition between environments

More on these features can be found at `https://docs.docker.com/compose/#features`.

Installing Docker-Compose

Mac and Windows users that have installed Docker Desktop can skip the installation step because Compose is included with the installed package.

1) For Linux users, run this command to download the current stable release of Docker Compose:

```
<code>
sudo curl -L "https://github.com/docker/compose/releases/
download/1.29.1/docker-compose-$(uname -s)-$(uname -m)" -o /
usr/local/bin/docker-compose
</code>
```

2) Apply executable permissions to the binary.

```
<code>
sudo chmod +x /usr/local/bin/docker-compose
</code>
```

Note   If the command `docker-compose` fails after installation, check your path. You can also create a symbolic link to `/usr/bin` or any other directory in your path.

For example,

```
<code>
sudo ln -s /usr/local/bin/docker-compose /usr/bin/
docker-compose
</code>
```

Optionally, install command completion for the bash and zsh shells. Test the installation.

```
<code>
$ docker-compose --version
</code>
```

The Development Environment

Now that you have Docker installed and ready to go, you need the YAML files for your project to set up your development environment. Go to `https://github.com/apress/php8-basics` and click the Download ZIP button, shown in Figure 1-5.

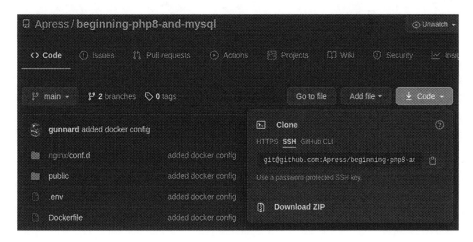

Figure 1-5. yaml files for your project

Once you have the ZIP file downloaded, unzip it in a directory of your choosing. We used ~/ (my users home directory) ~/coding. Once unzipped, your directory structure should look something like Figure 1-6.

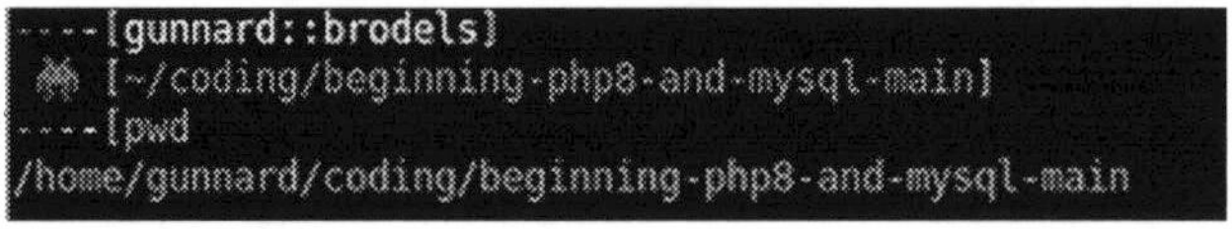

Figure 1-6. *Unzipped project folder*

Inside this directory will be all the information needed for Docker to start the development environment.

Go ahead and run

```
<code>
docker-compose up
</code>
```

and watch Docker spin up (Figure 1-7).

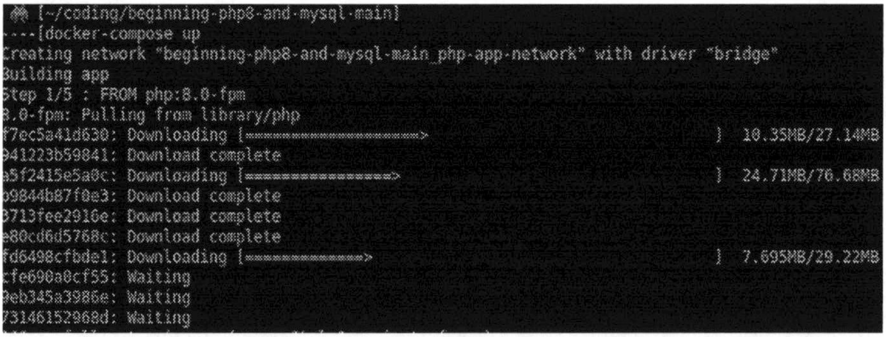

Figure 1-7. *Running the docker-compose command*

Next, point your browser to

```
<code>
http://localhost:8000
</code>
```

and you should see the table of contents page for this book and verification that the database has connected successfully. Go to the command prompt and type

```
<code>
docker ps
</code>
```

This command shows you any containers that Docker has or is currently using. Here you can see the mysql, nginx, and beginning php containers. One last thing to verify is that you can run PHP from within the PHP container. From the command line, type

```
<code>
docker exe -ti php-app bash
</code>
```

This connects you, much like ssh, to the container itself. From here, go into the Chapter1 directory.

```
<code>
cd Chapter1
</code>
```

Type

```
<code>
php first_script.php
</code>
```

You should see this output:

```
<code>
Output here
</code>
```

Summary

In this chapter, you learned in general the why, what, and how of using the PHP programming language in the development world. We introduced why you want to use PHP, Nginx, and MySQL and their benefits. As next steps, you learned how to install the Docker tool, which is an open platform for developing, shipping, and running applications. Finally, you saw why you needed the YAML files for your project to set up your development environment.

In the next chapter, we will explain how programming languages use variables to store and manipulate data and to build useful tools in PHP.

CHAPTER 2

PHP Fundamentals

In order to build useful tools in PHP, you need to know how to manipulate data. Programming languages use variables to store and manipulate data.

In this chapter, you will learn how programming languages use variables to store and manipulate data and to build useful tools in PHP.

Additionally, you'll explore the following topics:

- Using errors as tools

- Objects

- Verbs: GET and POST

Variables

PHP has a few rules when it comes to variables:

- A variable must start with the $ sign, followed by the name of the variable.

- A variable name must start with a letter or the underscore character.

- A variable name cannot start with a number.

- A variable name can only contain alpha-numeric characters and underscores (A-z, 0-9, and _).

- Variable names are case-sensitive ($pants and $PANTS are two different variables).

G. Engebreth and S. K. Sahu, *PHP 8 Basics*, https://doi.org/10.1007/978-1-4842-8082-9_2

Unlike other programming languages, PHP does not have a specific command for declaring variables. You must pay attention to where and how variables are declared and used.

Let's write some code and see how the browser handles it. Go into your beginning-php8-and-mysql directory and under chapter 2, create a file called newtest.php. Inside of this file, write

```
<code>
<p>this is normal text</p>
<?php
echo '<p>This is created by php';
?>
<p>this is normal text again</p>
</code>
```

The code above shows three lines. The first is normal HTML, the second is running PHP code, rendering HTML. The third is more HTML but after/outside the PHP code snippet. You can go between PHP and HTML as many times as you like within a .php file. This can get messy, so you want to limit this to very clean and precise code elements. Now create a file called vartest.php and open it up. Type this code into the file and save it:

```
<code>
<?php
echo "<p>variable test</p>";
$color = "blue";
$item = "pants";
echo "Today I am using $item which happen to be the color $color";
</code>
```

Navigate to localhost:8000/chapter2/vartest.php and look at the results (Figure 2-1).

variable test

Today I am using pants which happen to be the color blue

Figure 2-1. *URL result web page*

Ok, let's catch up on what you are doing here. First, you are declaring the PHP script with

```
<code>
<?php
</code>
```

The next line you use echo. This is a PHP command that makes up one of the most basic ways to display text from PHP to the browser. It does one thing: sends output to the browser or command prompt. Notice that after echo, you use the double quote (") as the delimiter to separate this portion of text and begin the line of text you wish to output to the screen. When you are done with the text, you end it with another double quote. The double quote is the delimiter that marks the beginning and end of a line of text you want to use. As humans, we can easily determine text or a sentence that is written down or on a screen. Computers need special markings, delimiters in this case, to determine where the text boundaries are. This is true for the echo command or for setting a variable, as in the next line. $color is the name of a variable you want to use and "blue" is the value you are setting it to. In this particular case, $color is a variable of type string. A string is any text that you want to use that will not be used to compute, say, a mathematical value. Once you have the value of "blue" set in $color, you can use echo to display it on the page. You do this again with the variable $item when you set its value to "pants". You will notice as well that each line of code ends with a semicolon (;). In PHP, this is how you tell the interpreter to stop reading the line and move on. You will get an error any time you leave out the ending semicolon.

17

Speaking of errors, let's go ahead and get comfortable with errors and how they can be useful to us instead of annoyances.

Using Errors As Tools

In PHP, you do not always see the errors that occur. This is because there are three different levels with configurations for how and where to display them. Let's go back into vartest.php and add these lines to the top:

```php
<?php
error_reporting( E_ALL );
ini_set( "display_errors", 1);

//this next line is an error
echo "these pretzels are making me thirsty;

echo "<p>variable test</p>";
$color = "blue";
$item = "pants";
echo "Today I am using $item which happen to be the color
$color";
```

Before you run this, let's explain what you are doing.

error_reporting(E_ALL); is telling PHP to display ALL errors. Here is the full list of options available for error_reporting:

```php
<?php

// Turn off all error reporting
error_reporting(0);

// Report simple running errors
error_reporting(E_ERROR | E_WARNING | E_PARSE);
```

```
// Reporting E_NOTICE can be good too (to report uninitialized
// variables or catch variable name misspellings ...)
error_reporting(E_ERROR | E_WARNING | E_PARSE | E_NOTICE);

// Report all errors except E_NOTICE
error_reporting(E_ALL & ~E_NOTICE);

// Report all PHP errors
error_reporting(E_ALL);

// Report all PHP errors
error_reporting(-1);

// Same as error_reporting(E_ALL);
ini_set('error_reporting', E_ALL);
```

The next line of ini_set() is used in PHP to overwrite configuration options that are set in the php.ini file. This is helpful when you need to do one-off configurations or are on a server where you do not have access to the ini file. The next line is the error line. Do you see it? Go ahead and pull up the file in your browser and see what it says.

```
<code>
Parse error: syntax error, unexpected token ">" in /var/www/
chapter2/vartest.php on line 8
</code>
```

Using this error, you can begin to hunt down the bug. This error is saying that line 8 has an unexpected >. Take a look at line 8 of your code:

```
<code>
echo "<p>variable test</p>";
</code>
```

This line looks perfectly fine to me. What PHP is telling us is that you have done something, in this case set a delimiter for text, on the line BEFORE line 8 and now the perfectly acceptable > on line 8 is unexpected. You need to look at line 6 where you will find the closing delimiter of " missing at the end of your text. Go ahead and add " to the end of the line and refresh your page, which should now render with no errors.

Now that you can create and assign variables, render text to the screen, and trigger/understand errors that show up, let's start building some pages. This is the reason you picked up this book, right? Go back to your Chapter2 directory and open the file main.php.

```
<code>
<?php
error_reporting( E_ALL );
ini_set( "display_errors",1);
$title = "Beginning PHP 8 & MySQL";
$content = "Here is the main content for this page";

$html ="
<!doctype html>

<html lang='en'><?php

<head>
  <meta charset='utf-8'>

  <title>$title</title>
  <meta name='description' content='Basic HTML5 Page'>
  <meta name='author' content='Your name'>

  <link rel='stylesheet' href='css/styles.css?v=1.0'>

</head>
```

```
<body>
$content
</body>
</html>";

echo $html;
</code>
```

These are the basic elements needed for a HTML 5 webpage with PHP included. You are declaring that you want errors to be turned on at the top, as you have done before. The next lines set two variables, one for the title and one for the content. The rest of the file sets the variable $html to the entirety of HTML that you want displayed on the page. Within this code you see the $title and $content variables placed where you want to display them on the page. Go ahead and open your browser to this page to see how it looks. This can get a little redundant if you have many pages that follow the same look and feel presented with the HTML. Therefore, you will use this page as a template that you can call and just switch out the values you want displayed. Open up main2.php in your editor.

```
<code>
<?php
//error_reporting( E_ALL );
//ini_set( "display_errors",1);
$title = "Beginning PHP 8 & MySQL";
$content = "Here is the main content for this page";
$html =include_once "inc/template2.php";
</code>
```

Here you are introducing the include_once function. By calling include_once, you tell PHP that you want to load a specific file into this area. By separating out the design aspect (HTML) from the PHP, you can view your code better and reuse the HTML elements in other PHP files.

Building on this example, let's take it a step further and include multiple PHP files in your template. In main2.php, change template.php to template2.php and refresh the page.

In your case, you first include header.php, located within the inc/ directory. When you use this method of including PHP snippets around the HTML in your file, you are essentially creating a template. This template (main.php), if used in another file, will still include a header, contents, and footer. Let's create a file called second.php by copying the main.php file and naming it second.php.

Now that you have come to an understanding with your templates on how to separate them and use them to your advantage, let's take a look at your variables. So far you have been using variables for trivial content, colors, and item names. What if you want to store someone's name and address? It's perfectly correct to do something like this:

```
<code>
$firstName = "gunnard";
$lastName = "engebreth";
</code>
```

This works fine until you want to start passing this information around between functions in your program. Basically, envision passing your friend a handful of Skittles vs. a bag of Skittles. Your friend still gets the Skittles in the end, but one way is clean, optimized, and all Skittles are guaranteed to reach your friend. This brings us to objects.

Objects

In PHP, an object is a specific set of data as defined in a class. In the code example above, you would say that the information would belong to a class of User. You would define that class as such:

```
<code>
```

```php
<?php
   class UserClass
      /* User variables */
      var $firstName;
      var $LastName;

      /* Member functions */
      function setFirstName($firstName){
         $this->firstName = $firstName;
      }

      function getFirstName(){
         echo $this->firstName;
      }

      function setLastName($lastName){
         $this->lastName = $lastName;
      }

      function getLastName(){
         echo $this->lastName;
      }
   }
   </code>
```

To create a new user you can call
```php
<code>
$user = new UserClass();
$user->setFirstName('gunnard');
$user->setLastName('engebreth');
var_dump($user);
</code>
```

Let's take a look at this code.

$user = new UserClass(); does exactly what it shows: the variable $user is now going to have the configuration and format that you described in the class UserClass. This also demonstrates the importance of proper naming in PHP. With one look at this line of code, you can have a high percentage of certainty that this variable $user is most likely going to be associated with $UserClass somehow and less likely to be associated with a class named $DumpTruckClass.

The next two lines call a method (function) you create within UserClass. These specific types of methods, Get____ and Set___, are known as helpers and also commonly referred to as the class "getters" and "setters." These methods simplify the task of setting values within the object.

The last line is a PHP-specific function used heavily in debugging code. var_dump() shows you exactly what is in a variable and what type of variable you are analyzing. In your example, calling var_dump shows all the information within the object. $user is the bag of Skittles and $user->firstName is the individual Skittle.

Now, how do you use this all together? You need to specify the class information in one file and include it in another file. Thankfully, you already know how to do that. Let's open up main3.php.

```
<code>
<?php
$title = "main3 php file";
require "UserClass.php";
$user = new UserClass;
$user->setFirstName = 'gunnard';
$user->setLastName = 'engebreth';
var_dump($user);
error_reporting( E_ALL );
ini_set( "display_errors",1);
$html =include_once "inc/template2.php";
</code>
```

You have already reviewed what the first two lines do, so set up and set the variable $user as a part of the class UserClass. The next two lines set the first name and last name. If you run this script on the command line or browser, you can verify this through the var_dump() function. Figure 2-2 shows what you should see.

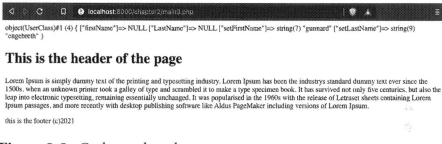

Figure 2-2. *Code result web page*

This is a fundamental stage in development. You have created an object, assigned values, and can display the information on the page. Now you need to make it dynamic by adding user interaction via forms.

Forms are more than just what you use to comment on someone's picture on Facebook. Forms are the method by which a user can interact with a program. The user can directly communicate with the code and the database you have created. With this kind of access, great detail must be put into validation and sanitization of input, which we will get to later. For now, just get comfortable with getting and using input. Let's get technical about receiving data from the user.

Verbs: GET and POST

HTTP (Hyper Text Transfer Protocol) is what connects the Web that you know today. This is the protocol or method of agreed-upon communication that allows for servers, PHP, and users to talk to one another. There are a lot of specifications within HTTP for everything including error handling, expected standard document formats, and request methods. These methods are defined in five verbs:

GET

> The GET method requests a representation of the specified resource. Requests using GET should only retrieve data.

POST

> The POST method is used to submit an entity to the specified resource, often causing a change in state or side effects on the server.

PUT

> The PUT method replaces all current representations of the target resource with the request payload.

DELETE

> The DELETE method deletes the specified resource.

PATCH

> The PATCH method is used to apply partial modifications to a resource.

You will be focusing on GET and POST but rest assured, you will be using the others as you build your REST API.

Point your browser to http://localhost:8000/chapter2/main4. php?pants=123. Notice in the URL you have main4.php?pants=123. When the page loads, it should look like Figure 2-3.

array(1) { ["pants"]=> string(3) "123" }

This is the header of the page

Lorem Ipsum is simply dummy text of the printing and typesetting industry. Lorem Ipsum has been the industrys standard dummy text ever since the 1500s, when an unknown printer took a galley of type and scrambled it to make a type specimen book. It has survived not only five centuries, but also the leap into electronic typesetting, remaining essentially unchanged. It was popularised in the 1960s with the release of Letraset sheets containing Lorem Ipsum passages, and more recently with desktop publishing software like Aldus PageMaker including versions of Lorem Ipsum.

this is the footer (c)2021

Figure 2-3. *URL result web page*

At the top is var_dump() and you can see that the info you have in the URL is now available to you in PHP as the variable $userVars. This is available to you through the HTTP verb GET and in PHP you use the global variable $_GET. GET specifically allows for the transfer of data through the URL. You can send multiple values as well. Change the URL to include

```
http://localhost:8000/chapter2/main4.php?pants=123&dog=poodle&food=spaghetti
```

Refresh the page and you will now see that Pants, Dog, and Food have values set to them. The other method of transmitting data from the user to your code is using POST.

The POST verb behaves in nearly the same way but does not use the URL, thereby keeping the data you are transmitting a bit more secure. In order to see the POST functionality, open main5.php and take a look.

```
<?php
$userVars = $_POST;
$title = "main5 php file";
require "UserClass.php";
$user = new UserClass;
$user->setFirstName = 'gunnard';
$user->setLastName = 'engebreth';
```

27

```
var_dump($userVars);
error_reporting( E_ALL );
ini_set( "display_errors",1);
$html =include_once "inc/template3.php";
</code>
```

The main things that changed in this code are that you are using the PHP global $_POST instead of $_GET and you include template3.php. Let's look at the tempalte3.php file.

```
<code>
$content = include('contentPost.php');
</code>
```

Template3 calls in a specific content piece called contentPost.php.

```
<code>
<form action="<?php echo htmlspecialchars($_SERVER["PHP_
SELF"]);?>" method="post">
<input type="text" id="firstName" name="firstName" />
<input type="text" id="lastName" name="lastName" />
<input type="submit" name="submit">
</code>
```

Here you see the differences in that allow you to use $_POST. You define a form and set the action to the file (main5.php) itself. This code you see allows for the form to be used in multiple places by dynamically finding the name of the file that houses the form and putting it there. $_SERVER['PHP_SELF'] is the file currently calling this script and htmlspecialchars is a PHP function that removes HTML because it can be used for malicious or evil intent. The two lines underneath declare the firstname and lastname boxes to collect the users input. Finally, you have a Submit button that triggers the form to be used by your code. Go ahead and fill it out and then look at the resulting page (Figure 2-4).

Figure 2-4. Code result web page

You can see in your var_dump that the variables for first name and last name came through, and if you look at your URL, you see that it is clean and no variables are listed. In your examples, you used GET and POST to submit data to your PHP. Technically, you could use GET to submit this form as well, but you should really not do that. These two methods, GET and POST, are (as listed above) part of a larger group of verbs that are used currently in modern development in APIs. An application programming interface (API) is a method of allowing access for developers to interact with an application. Think about it this way: stock tickers, tweet streams, an Instagram plugin for WordPress-- these all are individual pieces of software that connect to other things:

- Stock ticker -> Bloomberg API

- Tweet stream -> Twitter API

- Instagram gallery -> Instagram API

The software will send specifically formatted (typically JSON or XML) data to the API, which will authenticate the software's access and return the requested data. The software will then take that data, and read and reformat it into a useable form. Referring back to the API verbs above, the software will send a GET request to an API and expect back a response with the requested data. This is the stock, Twitter, or Instagram information we spoke about. Software can then POST data to the API in order to create or start a process. A POST request is used to create a new Twitter account or to actually make a trade with Bloomberg. PUT and PATCH can be used as "update" methods that can alter a users' status or swap out profile pictures, for example. DELETE is primarily used to remove or destroy data from the API. While it is completely possible to only use GET and POST for an API, the separation of verbs and (as you will see) routes based off of these verbs will allow for a much easier and better experience for the developer using the given API. If you are using POST to create, update, delete, and search, this can get messy because you will need to not only look at whether the request is GET/POST but now also a new variable needs to be set to specify the intended action (create, update, delete, search, etc.). Clear and direct methods of communication not only help humans communicate but can keep things straightforward with software, too.

Summary

Let's review the ideas you've learned so far.

1) Variables store information for PHP to use. This information can be set within the code by the developer or received from outside by the user. Variables start with a $ and should be named something relevant to their purpose.

2) PHP and HTML can be intermixed. It is acceptable to use PHP within HTML through opening and closing PHP with <?php and ?>. Keeping the code clean and readable should be a priority.

3) echo prints out text or variables

4) Errors should be embraced as tools for debugging. Errors can be turned on/off and configured through

   a. error_reporting(E_ALL);

   b. ini_set("display_errors", 1);

5) `include_once()` allows you to pull in code from another file, enabling you to separate out PHP and HTML into separate files.

6) PHP objects allow you to group sets of information into one container or object.

7) `GET` and `POST` are used to receive user input. `GET` is transferred through the URL in plain text and `POST` is not.

8) `GET` and `POST` are two of the five verbs commonly used by APIs to communicate.

In the next chapter, you will learn how to declare and use classes and functions (including traits, which is what a class is to an object). Also, object-oriented programming (OOP) will be explained.

CHAPTER 3

Functions, Classes, and Traits

So far, you have been using PHP for simple top-down scripting.

In this chapter, you will learn how to declare and use classes and functions (including class definitions, visibility, inheritance, and traits). Also, object-oriented programming (OOP) will be introduced and explained.

The real power of PHP comes with the ability to declare and use classes and functions. As a quick overview, classes are (as you saw in the last chapter) definitions for objects to use when being created. The class definitions then turn into objects that you can use to store and manipulate data. Functions are reserved words within PHP that you declare, define, and call in order to do small or complex tasks. The reason you separate out these tasks into functions is so that you can abstract them and their usage. Abstract is a fancy way of allowing for a function to be called by multiple sources for one purpose. Instead of writing a function in multiple classes to do the exact same thing, you can set that function apart in a class and call it whenever you need. The duplication of code is one thing to look out for when refactoring or even working through your logic.

With these concepts in mind, this chapter will focus on the world of OOP, which models the application and development around real-world objects such as users, cars, colors, or even vegetables.

© Gunnard Engebreth, Satej Kumar Sahu 2023
G. Engebreth and S. K. Sahu, *PHP 8 Basics*, https://doi.org/10.1007/978-1-4842-8082-9_3

This chapter will cover the following topics:

- Object-oriented programming (OOP)

- Class definitions

- Class visibility

- Class inheritance

- Polymorphism and abstract classes

OOP

The three basic concepts in object-oriented programming are

- **Encapsulation**: This is concerned with the optics or exposure of information between classes and the rest of the application. The benefits of this include

  - **Complexity reduction**: Data that is not needed outside of certain classes is not available outside of those classes.

  - **Data protection**: Allowing access to data through GET/SET methods creates a flexible and maintainable codebase.

- **Polymorphism**: The ability to have one form of data structure with multiple uses and implementations

  - Class extension and abstraction allow for this.

- **Inheritance**: Classes have the ability to share information between each other depending on visibility and the parent/child relationship.

These concepts are more than just a specific method of declaring methods and properties. This is about thinking, structure, data flow, and coding methodology. It's comparable to the difference between knowing the rules of chess and knowing what a London opening is and how to defend yourself. These concepts drive how you think about data, usage, and manipulation. While object-oriented programming can be taught, it is best learned through hands-on development. OOP might seem rigid and forceful at first, but there will come a time where the freedom and creativity that come from defining, extending, and abstracting make sense and begins to drive your development process.

Reviewing Class Definitions

Let's review the class definition from above:

```
<code>
<?php
   class UserClass
{
     /* User variables */
     var $firstName;
     var $LastName;

     /* Member functions */
     function setFirstName($firstName){
        $this->firstName = $firstName;
     }

     function getFirstName(){
        echo $this->firstName;
     }

     function setLastName($lastName){
        $this->lastName = $lastName;
     }
```

```
       function getLastName(){
          echo $this->lastName;
       }
    }
</code>
```

Class definitions begin with the PHP keyword class followed by the name and then a pair of curly braces. Within these curly braces is where the properties (variables) and methods (functions) belonging to the class are defined. Within classes, functions are referred to as methods. This is a whisky/bourbon situation. All bourbon is whiskey, but not all whisky is bourbon. All methods are functions, but not all functions you see are methods. The name of the class, in your case UserClass, has a few restrictions as to how it can be named:

- It can't be a reserved word.

- It must start with a letter or underscore.

PHP has many reserved words. You have already seen class, function, and any PHP function such as var_dump or echo used in PHP. These words cannot be reused as variables or names for what is dubbed "userland" use. Any class, method, function, or variable created by a user and not built into PHP is deemed "userland." This is not necessarily as derogatory as it may sound but just a way of keeping the two worlds separate. In your example, you have variable declarations for

```
<code>
 /* User variables */
       var $firstName;
       var $LastName;
</code>
```

Class Visibility

Class properties and methods have what is referred to as visibility. This visibility can be defined by prefixing the declaration of the property. For example,

```
<code>
public $firstName = 'Abraham';
protected $lastName = 'lincolin';
private $nickName = 'beardyface';
</code>
```

In the example class above, you use var to declare your property, which defaults to public. The reasoning for visibility levels is for control over how data flows within your code. PHP allow you to do something like this:

```
<code>
$user = getUser($userId);

function showUserName() {
    $user = getUser(4);
    var_dump($user);
}
var_dump($user);
showUserName();
</code>
```

Here you are getting quite sloppy with your variables and logic, and PHP is trusting that you know what you are doing. PHP provides three levels to keep internal function variables and external variables separate from one another: public, protected, and private.

Public

Public properties have no restrictions for calling them in any scope. This means that a public property of an object can both be retrieved and also modified anywhere in code. As stated, this is the default behavior when declaring a class property using var. While this is acceptable in terms of functional PHP code, you should define the visibility of a property when it is declared.

Protected

The second level is protected, which means that the class that they are declared in or any class that extends them can access the property.

Private

The last level, private, is like protected but takes it up a notch by only allowing access to the class it is defined in. Any subclass or extended class cannot access this property.

There is more to visibility, such as making properties and methods MORE visible and extending them as well. These topics are for another day but if you wish to read up on them, php.net has great information on all things visibility.

A Closer Look at Class Inheritance

Inheritance in PHP is specifically from a parent class to a child class. A child class can inherit any public or protected properties or methods that have been defined in their parent class. Inheritance occurs when a new class "extends" the previous parent class. For example, you can extend your UserClass class from before.

```
<code>
```

```
class RegisteredUser extends UserClass {
    function  setRegistrationNumber($number) {
        $this->registrationNumber = $number;
    }
    function getRegistrationNumber() {
        return $this->registrationNumber;
    }
}

$currentUser = new RegisteredUser();
$currentUser->setFirstName('Robert');
$currentUser->setLastName('Paulson');
$currentUser->setRegistrationNumber('1234xyz');
</code>
```

As you see, currentUser, having been based or "extended" from UserClass, has access to the methods setFirstName and setLastName. currentUser is being extended with setRegistrationNumber, allowing you to extend the class specifications of UserClass.

In other words, extending a class is the equivalent to adding guacamole to an already existing type of burrito. If you order a #2 burrito from the menu, it already has its ingredients defined and set. This is like your parent class, UserClass. Now, by adding on a non-predefined ingredient, you are extending the burrito. The burrito is essentially the same but with something more that you specified. Rightly so, the restaurant can't call this burrito a #2 anymore, because it is not, and it needs to name it something else, like you have done with RegisteredUser. RegisteredUser is essentially the same as UserClass but with something extra, something that you have defined. Extending does not end with the entire class, but anything that is public or protected. Properties (variables) and methods (functions) can all be extended as long as the class visibility allows for it.

Now let's talk about polymorphism by looking at abstract classes.

Polymorphism and Abstract Classes

Unlike extending a class, an abstract class is like a self-serve ice cream sundae bar. You declare that you want an ice cream sundae but all you have is an empty container. Until you put in the ice cream and all the toppings you want, it is not a complete sundae. Either way, you create a new sundae and at the end a new sundae is what you get. The ability to customize the object (sundae) is what makes it abstract. With abstract classes, you can define in the parent class a method name and properties but you allow for the child class to define what the method actually does. This also creates the dependency on the child class to define this method. Let's take a look:

```
<code>
<?php
// Parent class
abstract class Candy {
  public $name;
  public function __construct($name) {
    $this->name = $name;
  }
  abstract public function slogan() : string;
}

// Child classes
class Skittle extends Candy {
  public function slogan() : string {
    return "$this->name! - Taste the rainbow!";
  }
}

class Twix extends Candy {
  public function slogan() : string {
```

```php
      return "$this->name - Which side are you?";
   }
}

class KitKat extends Candy {
   public function slogan() : string {
      return "$this->name - Gimmie a break!";
   }
}

// Create objects from the child classes
$skittle = new Skittle('Skittles');
echo $skittle->slogan();

$kitkat = new KitKat('KitKat');
echo $kitkat->slogan();
?>
</code>
```

In this example, you define the abstract parent class Candy with a property for the name and two methods. The construct method is standard and takes a string for name. The second is the slogan method, which is (for all intents and purposes) empty and returns a string. What you are doing with this is carving out the name slogan in the class but allowing the child classes to define what that method is actually doing. You are keeping consistency within the objects you create by doing this. As long as the object is created from a class that extends Candy, you know that there is a slogan method, and if you are the one that extends the class, you know that you need to define what this method does.

Constants

Classes also can have constants. Constants are properties or methods that can be defined within a class and used (depending on visibility) from anywhere.

```php
<code>
<?php
class MessageClass {
  const EXIT_MESSAGE = "Thank you for coming to my
  TEDDY talk!";
  public function thankyouBye() {
    echo self::EXIT_MESSAGE;
  }
}

$byebye = new MessageClass();
$byebye->thankyouBye();
?>

"Thank you for coming to my TEDDY talk!"
</code>
```

There are two ways in which this constant can be accessed. From within the class, self:: can be used, which you did in your example. The other way is to reference the class name and the double ::, such as MessageClass::EXIT_MESSAGE. Constants can be useful in the organization of properties and ensuring continuity of values across your application. In your example, you have a message class to house all of your application messages. This way you only have one class to call and one class to ever change if there is a need to update a message. If there are one-off messages, you can always extend the class and adjust the verbiage from there. The main point of using constants in this way is to keep your data structured and organized for the best use as you develop and to keep the duplication of code down to a minimum. There is no need for multiple variables with the same "welcome" message if you can set it in one class and reference it from anywhere.

Constructs

Classes offer constructors and destructors. The former is called and "constructs" at the time a new object is created and the latter "destructs" as soon as there are no other references to a particular object. A constructor method looks like this:

```
<code>
<?php
class UserClass {
    function __construct() {
        print "In UserClass constructor\n";
    }
}
</code>
```

Note that the construct() method has __ in front of the name. Prior to PHP 8, classes with a method named the same as the class would interpret that method as the constructor. This will now result in an E_DEPRECATED error but still run as a constructor. If both __construct() and a method with the same name as the class are defined, __construct() will be called.

Constructors are used to set certain parameters to properties when new objects are created. This can easily be done now in PHP 8 with constructor property promotion.

```
<code>
<?php
class Point {
    public function __construct(
```

```
        protected int $x,
        protected int $y = 0
)
    {

    }
}
</code>
```

A destructor method would look like the following:

```
<code>
<?php
class UserClass {
    function __destruct() {
        print "Destroying " . __CLASS__ ."\n";
}
}
</code>
```

While this destructor only prints the status `Destroying UserClass`, a more practical use is to clear the cache, `unset()` variables, or other housekeeping items.

Traits

Then there are traits. Think about a trait as what a class is to an object, the trait is to a class. You can define several methods in a trait and use them in several different classes as long as the classes reference back to the trait. The reason you use traits in PHP is because PHP is a single inheritance language. This means that while you can define a class and all of its methods and any subclass you extend from that will have access to those methods, you can't reach over to another class and borrow a method.

The subclass cannot inherit methods from another class. To prevent you from duplicating code all over the place, you can reference a trait from multiple subclasses to utilize a single method. Here is a simple example:

```
<code>
<?php
trait userFunctions {
    public function message1() {
        echo "user message1";
    }
}

class UserClass {
    use userFunctions;
}

class UserClass2 {
    use userFunctions;
}

$user = new UserClass();
$user2 = new UserClass2();
$user->message1();
$user2->message1();
</code>
```

This prints out the message "user message1 user message1" from two separate classes. This is very useful when dealing with large systems that share functionality but not necessarily the same data.

Lastly, we must discuss namespaces and their function within OOP.

Namespaces

Namespaces allow for the labeling of classes so that when you reference them within your code, you can specify the class you wish to use from within its namespace. You can also use namespaces to group together classes for better organization. Namespaces also allow for the use of the same name in different classes. Here is how a namespace is declared:

```
<code>
<?php
namespace Pants;
</code>
```

A namespace declaration must be the first code within a PHP file. Everything after the namespace declaration is considered within this namespace.

```
<code>
<?php
Namespace Pants;

class PantsMaker {
        $color = 'blue';
        $size = 'large';

        public function pantsLabel($name) {
        $label = "These pants are size: $size , color: $color
        named: $name";
           return $label;
    }
}

$thesePants = new Pants();
echo $thesePants->pantsLabel('leeevi');
</code>
```

From a file outside of the Pants class declaration, the code would look like this:

```
<code>
<?php

$thesePants = new Pants\PantsMaker();
echo $thesePants->pantsLabel('leeevi');
</code>
```

You can also just include this PHP file within the same namespace and there is no need for the beginning Pants\.

```
<code>
<?php
namespace Pants;
$thesePants = new PantsMaker();
echo $thesePants->pantsLabel('leeevi');
</code>
```

There is also the ability to alias a namespace for ease of use or better code management.

```
<code>
namespace Pants as P;
$thesePants = new P\PantsMaker();
echo $thesePants->pantsLabel('leeevi');
</code>
```

There is a lot more to cover in terms of PHP objects and OOP in general. This is but a small glance. We highly recommend seeking out more information on OOP and what PHP has to offer.

Summary

Let's review what you now know about OOP.

- OOP consists of three concepts:

    - **Encapsulation**: Keeping functionality within the specific class, separated from where it is not needed

    - **Polymorphism**: Allowing for multiple versions to be created from one parent class

    - **Inheritance**: The sharing of specific properties and methods from parent to child

- Classes are used to define objects.

- Objects use properties and methods defined in classes to handle data.

- Classes can extend one another in a parent-child relationship.

- Classes use visibility (public, private, or protected) to allow extended classes to share properties and methods.

- Classes can be abstract, allowing child classes to define how methods or properties work at the time they are created.

In the next chapter, you will learn how to work with data and data types such as Bool, Int, Float, and Array.

CHAPTER 4

Data and Data Types

In this chapter, you will learn how PHP deals with data and data types and how variables are used to store data in PHP, from simple strings and numbers to more complicated arrays and objects.

A data type is how you classify data into a certain category according to its attributes, which can be

- **Alphanumeric**: Where characters are classified as strings

- **Whole numbers**: Which are classified integers

- **Floating points**: Which are numbers with decimal points

- **Boolean**: Which can be true or false

This chapter will cover the following topics:

- Introduction of PHP data types

- Scalar types (predefined)

- Compound types (user-defined)

- Special types

PHP Data Types

In general, PHP supports eight basic data types used to create variables, and depending on what type of data you wish to store, you choose the appropriate variable of that data type. If you wish to store the phrase "Hello

G. Engebreth and S. K. Sahu, *PHP 8 Basics*, https://doi.org/10.1007/978-1-4842-8082-9_4

World" within a variable, you choose the type string over the type integer. Why? A string is a sequence of characters while an integer is a non-decimal number between -2,147,483,648 and 2,147,483,647. For practicality purposes, using a string makes more sense, and if you try to assign "Hello World" to an integer, PHP will kindly tell you that you cannot do such a thing.

Here are the eight basic data types used to create variables in PHP:

- Scalar types (predefined):
  - Boolean
  - Integer
  - Float
  - String
- Compound types (user-defined):
  - Array
  - Object
- Special types:
  - NULL
  - Resource

PHP Data Types: Scalar Types

In PHP, scalar means

1) A quantity, such as mass, length, or speed, that is completely specified by its magnitude and has no direction

2) A number, numerical quantity, or element in a field

3) A device that yields an output equal to the input multiplied by a constant, as in a linear amplifier

You can consider a number like 10 or 5 as a scalar. A word, letter, or phrase such as "Hello World" is considered a scalar as well.

This PHP data type holds only a single value and includes four scalar data types:

- Boolean

- Integer

- Float

- String

Boolean

A bool or boolean type is the simplest type. Bool expresses a "truth" value of either true or false.

To specify a bool literal, use the constants true or false. Both are case-insensitive.

```php
<?php
$foo = True; // set the value TRUE to $foo
?>
```

Booleans are often used in conditional testing, such as

```php
<?php
if ($isTuesday) {
    echo "Taco Tuesday!!";
}
?>
```

Integer

An int is a non-decimal number between -2,147,483,648 and 2,147,483,647.
Integers can be specified in four different bases:

1) Decimal (base 10) [1, 2, 3, 4, 5, 6, etc.]

2) Hexadecimal (base 16) [1A, 1B, 1C, etc.]

3) Ocatal (base 8) [1, 2, 3, 4, 5, 6, 7]

4) Binary (base 2) [0, 1, 1011, etc.]

Integers must adhere to these rules as well:

- An integer must have at least one digit.

- An integer must not have a decimal point.

```php
<?php
$a = 1234; // decimal number
$a = 0123; // octal number (equivalent to 83 decimal)
$a = 0o123; // octal number (as of PHP 8.1.0)
$a = 0x1A; // hexadecimal number (equivalent to 26 decimal)
$a = 0b11111111; // binary number (equivalent to 255 decimal)
$a = 1_234_567; // decimal number (as of PHP 7.4.0)
?>
```

Float

A float (floating point number) is a number with a decimal point or a
number in exponential form.

```php
<?php
$a = 1.234;
$b = 1.2e3;
```

```
$c = 7E-10;
$d = 1_234.567; // as of PHP 7.4.0
?>
```

String

A string is a sequence of characters, like "Hello World!".

A string can be any text inside quotes. You can use single or double quotes.

```
<?php
$foo = "Hello World!";
$bar = 'Hello World!';
?>
```

A string literal can be specified in four different ways:

- Single quotes

- Double quotes

- Heredoc syntax

- Nowdoc syntax

The most basic way to specify a variable as a string is to enclose it in a single quote ('). If you want to specify an ACTUAL single quote for use, you need to "escape" the character itself or tell PHP to ignore the functionality of this character and just use the single quote as a real single quote you want to print out somewhere. The escape character for PHP is the backslash (\). This begs the questions, how do you escape a backslash in order to use a literal backslash. Simple. You escape it just the same, as in (\\). Unlike the other syntaxes for strings (double-quoted and heredoc), variables and escape sequences for special characters are not be expanded when using single-quoted strings.

```php
<?php
echo 'this is a single quoted string';

echo 'You can also have embedded newlines if
This is the best way
To get the job done';

// Outputs: that robot once said: "I'll be back"
echo 'that robot once said: "I\'ll be back"';

// Outputs: You formatted C:\*.*?
echo 'You formatted C:\\*.*?';

// Outputs: You formatted C:\*.*?
echo 'You formatted C:\*.*?';

// Outputs: This will not create: \n a newline
echo 'This will not create: \n a newline';

// Outputs: Variables also do not $expand
echo 'Variables also do not $expand';
?>
```

When using double quotes ("), PHP interprets the following escape sequences for special characters:

Sequence	Meaning
\n	Linefeed (LF or 0x0A (10) in ASCII)
\r	Carriage return (CR or 0x0D (13) in ASCII)
\t	Horizontal tab (HT or 0x09 (9) in ASCII)
\v	Vertical tab (VT or 0x0B (11) in ASCII)
\e	Escape (ESC or 0x1B (27) in ASCII)
\f	Form feed (FF or 0x0C (12) in ASCII)
\\	Backslash
\$	Dollar sign
\"	Double quote
\[0-7]{1,3}	The sequence of characters matching the regular expression is a character in octal notation, which silently overflows to fit in a byte (e.g., "\400" === "\000")
\x[0-9A-Fa-f]{1,2}	The sequence of characters matching the regular expression is a character in hexadecimal notation
\u{[0-9A-Fa-f]+}	The sequence of characters matching the regular expression is a Unicode codepoint, which will be output to the string as that codepoint's UTF-8 representation

The escape character for double-quoted strings is the same as single quotes; it is the backslash (\). The main difference between single and double-quoted strings is the fact that variables are expanded if they are used within double quotes.

A third method to create a string data type in PHP is with the heredoc syntax: <<< . This method is especially useful for large amounts of preformatted text. To use the heredoc, you simply start with this operator, <<<, and afterwards it is followed by an identifier that marks the name or reference of this string and then a newline. The string comes next and then the same identifier from the beginning is used to close or end the quotation. It looks something like this:

```php
<?php
 echo <<<MYIDENTIFIER
Here is
The text that
I want to display
MYIDENTIFIER;
?>
```

Text within a heredoc behaves just like a double-quoted string does. The escape codes above and quotes can still be used. Variables are expanded as well.

Also, the closing identifier must follow the same naming rules as any other label in PHP: it must contain only alphanumeric characters and underscores, and it must start with a non-digit character or underscore.

```php
<?php
echo <<<"FOOBAR"
Hello World!
FOOBAR;
?>
```

Nowdocs are the single-quoted version of heredocs. Nowdocs are specified in the same manner but the identifier is enclosed within single quotes.

```php
<?php
Echo <<<'FOOBAR'
Text that will not get parsed,
This will just show up
FOOBAR
?>
```

A string specified in double quotes or with heredoc has the variables within it parsed. There are two types of syntax that can be used for this: simple or complex. This does not describe the ease at which to use either one; rather, it describes the complexity of the variables that are being parsed. The simple syntax is most commonly used and provides a way to embed a variable, an array value, or an object property in a string with minimum effort. The complex syntax uses curly braces to organize and tell PHP what needs to be parsed.

```php
<?php
$tea = "earl grey";

echo "He drank some $tea tea.".PHP_EOL;
// Invalid. "s" is a valid character for a variable name, but
the variable is $tea.
echo "He drank some tea made of $teas.";
// Valid. Explicitly specify the end of the variable name by
enclosing it in braces:
echo "He drank some tea made of ${tea}.";
?>
```

This will output the following:

He drank some earl grey tea.

He drank some tea made of .

He drank some tea made of earl grey.

As stated before, complex syntax is not called complex because the syntax is complex, but because it allows for the use of complex expressions. With the complex syntax, any array element, scalar variable, or object property that has a string representation (variable with a string) can be included in this syntax. This means not only can you display a simple string via a variable named $foo = "bar" but you can display more complex situations such as $foo[$x] = "Bar".

This is valid syntax although some variables need to be defined first. Take a look at the following for the correct syntax:

```php
<?php
$great = 'fun';

// outputs: This is { fun}
echo "This is { $great}";

// outputs: This is fun
echo "This is {$great}";

// Works
echo "This square is {$square->width}00 centimeters broad.";

// Works, quoted keys only work using the curly brace syntax
echo "This works: {$arr['key']}";

// Works
echo "This works: {$arr[4][3]}";

// This is wrong for the same reason as $foo[bar] is
wrong  outside a string.
// In other words, it will still work, but only because PHP
first looks for a
// constant named foo; an error of level E_NOTICE (undefined
constant) will be
// thrown.
```

```php
echo "This is wrong: {$arr[foo][3]}";

// Works. When using multi-dimensional arrays, always use
braces around arrays
// when inside of strings
echo "This works: {$arr['foo'][3]}";

// Works.
echo "This works: " . $arr['foo'][3];

echo "This works too: {$obj->values[3]->name}";

echo "This is the value of the var named $name: {${$name}}";

echo "This is the value of the var named by the return value of
getName(): {${getName()}}";

echo "This is the value of the var named by the return value of
\$object->getName(): {${$object->getName()}}";

// Won't work, outputs: This is the return value of getName():
{getName()}
echo "This is the return value of getName(): {getName()}";

// Won't work, outputs: C:\folder\{fun}.txt
echo "C:\folder\{$great}.txt"
// Works, outputs: C:\folder\fun.txt
echo "C:\\folder\\{$great}.txt"
?>
```

Accessing class properties:

```php
<?php
class foo {
    var $bar = 'I am bar.';
}
```

```
$foo = new foo();
$bar = 'bar';
$baz = array('foo', 'bar', 'baz', 'quux');
echo "{$foo->$bar}\n";
echo "{$foo->{$baz[1]}}\n";
?>
```

PHP String Functions

PHP has many built-in functions specifically designed for strings, including

- substr()
- strlen()
- str_replace()
- trim()
- strpos()
- strtolower()
- strtoupper()
- is_string()
- strstr()

substr()

```
string substr(string string, int start[, int length] );
```

The return value is a substring copied from within the string.

```
$comment = 'your product works well!';
```

When calling the function, you can use either positive or negative numbers. A positive number gets the string from the start position to the end of the string. A negative start number gets the string from the end of the string minus the start characters to the end of the string. Look at chapter4-substring.php.

```
$comment = 'Your product is great!';
echo substr($comment, 1) . "\n";
//  returns 'Your product is great!'.

$comment = 'Your product is great!';
echo substr($comment, -9) . "\n";
//  returns 'is great!'
```

```
our product is great!
is great!
```

The length parameter is used to specify one of two things:

- Number of characters returned (positive length)
- The end character of the return sequence (negative length)

```
$comment = 'Your product is great!';
substr($comment, 0, 4);
// returns 'Your'

substr($comment, 5, -10);
//returns 'product'
```

5 signifies the starting character point (p) and -10 determines the ending point (count 10 places backwards starting from the end of the string).

strlen( )

strlen( ) is used for checking the length of a string.

```
echo strlen("Harder Faster Better Stronger");
// 29
```

```php
<?php
$foo = "bar";

if (strlen ( $foo ) > 0) {
    echo 'that is valid foo';
} else {
    echo 'that foo is too small';
}
?>

// that foo is too small
```

str_replace( )

Many times, with strings, being able to find and replace a substring is handy. With str_replace( ), this is made easy for us.

```
mixed str_replace(mixed needle, mixed new_needle, mixed
haystack[, int &count]));
```

str_replace( ) uses a common concept in PHP which is "needle" and "haystack". When you see this, you can think of the idea of finding a needle in a haystack. This lays out for you which term is which. I am looking for a needle in haystack, as in str_replace("pants", $longParagraph). To be clear:

"pants" == needle

$longParagraph == haystack

```php
<?php
$strings = array (
            'You like to have a snazzy time',
            'You are a really snazzy person',
            'Would you like to drink a cup of coffee?'
);

$search = array (
            'snazzy',
            'cup',
            'person',
            'coffee'
);
$replace = array (
            'great',
            'bottle'',
            'dude',
            'Dark brown stuff'
);

$replaced = str_replace ( $search, $replace, $strings );
```

trim( )

Dealing with unknown input is tricky, and this is where trim( ) comes in handy. The trim( ) function strips away unwanted spaces from the left, right, or both sides of a string. You can also specify which characters you would like to strip.

```php
<?php
$trimit = 'junk awesome stuff junk';

$trimmed = trim ( $trimit, 'junk' );
```

```
print_r ( $trimmed );

// awesome stuff
?>
```

strpos( )

The function `strpos()` operates in a similar fashion to `strstr()`, except, instead of returning a substring, it returns the numerical position of a needle within a haystack.

```
int strpos(string haystack, string needle, int [offset] );
```

The integer returned is the position of the first occurrence of the needle within the haystack. The first character is in position 0, just like arrays.

You can see by running the following code that your exclamation point is at position 13.

```
$awesome = "Super Awesome!";
echo strpos($awesome, "!");
```

```
// 13
```

This function accepts a single character as the needle, but it can accept a string of any length. The optional offset parameter determines the point within the haystack to start searching.

```
$awesome = "Super Awesome!";
echo strpos($awesome, 'm', 3);
// 11
```

This code echoes the value 11 to the browser because PHP started looking for the character m at position 3.

In any of these cases, if the needle is not in the string, `strpos()` will return false. To avoid strange behavior, you can use the === operator to test return values. See `chapter4-strpos.php`.

```php
<?php
$awesome = "Super Awesome!";

$result = strpos ( $awesome, 'G' );
if ($result === false) {
    echo 'Not found';
} else {
    echo 'Found at position ' . $result;
}

// Not found
?>
```

strtolower( )

Very often in PHP you need to compare strings or correct capitalization when people SHOUT or do odd things. In order to compare strings, you want to make sure they are the same case. You can use `strtolower()` for this purpose. Let's use a function created with `strtolower()` to calm down an angry person.

```php
<?php
function calm_down($string) {

    return strtolower ( $string );
}

$person = 'Angry people SHOUT!';
```

```php
echo calm_down ( $person );
// angry people shout!
?>
```

strtoupper( )

strtoupper( ) is also quite popular for many of the reasons listed above
but in reverse, meaning it takes a lowercase or mixed case string and sets it
to all upper case. Let's change things up and create a wake-up function to
get your workers going in the morning.

```php
<?php
function wake_up($string) {

    return strtoupper ( $string );
}

$person = 'these people need to get working!';

echo wake_up ( $person );
// THESE PEOPLE NEED TO GET WORKING!
?>
```

is_string( )

is_string( ) is used to check if a value is a string. Let's take a look at this
within an if( ) statement to take an action on strings in one way and non-
strings in another. is_string( ) returns true or false.

```php
<?php
if (is_string ( 7 )) {
    echo "Yes";
} else {
    echo "No";
```

```
}
// No

if (is_string ( "Lucky Number 7" )) {
    echo "Yes";
} else {
    echo "No";
}
// Yes
?>
```

strstr( )

Last but not least is the strstr() function. The function strstr() can be used to find a string or character match within a longer string. This function can be used to find a string inside a string, including finding a string containing only a single character.

```
string strstr(string haystack, string needle);
```

You pass strstr() a haystack to be searched and a needle to be found. If an exact match of the needle is found, the strstr() function returns the haystack from the needle onward. If it does not find the needle, it will return false. If the needle occurs more than once, the returned string will begin from the first occurrence of the needle.

As an example, let's say you have a submission form for people to submit their website, but you would like it in a certain format. You can use strstr() to check for a string within a string to help you here.

```
<?php
$url = 'vegibit.com';

if (strstr ( $url, 'https://www.' ) === false) {
    $url = 'http://www.' . $url;
```

```
}
echo $url;
// https://www.vegibit.com
?>
```

Two compound types:

I

In the next section, you'll walk through compound data types.

PHP Data Types: Compound Types

PHP compound types can hold multiple values and include two data types:

- Array

- Object

Array

An array in PHP is actually an ordered map. A map is a type that associates values to keys. This type is optimized for several different uses; it can be treated as an array, list (vector), hash table (an implementation of a map), dictionary, collection, stack, queue, and probably more. Since array values can be other arrays, trees and multidimensional arrays are also possible.

Explanations of these data structures are beyond the scope of this manual, but we'll provide at least one example for each of them. For more information, look for the considerable literature that exists about this broad topic.

An array in PHP is a type that associates values to keys. By default, PHP assigns the keys as numbers starting at 0 and going to the size of your array. See chapter4.php.

```
<?php
$myArray[0] = "first";
```

```
$myArray[1] = "Second";
$myArray[2] = "3rd";

var_dump($myArray);
?>

array(3) {
  [0]=>
  string(5) "first"
  [1]=>
  string(6) "second"
  [2]=>
  string(3) "3rd"
}
```

PHP also gives you the option to have specifically assigned keys that may have more meaning to your application. They are called associative arrays.

```
<?php

$myArray['fruit'] = "apple";
$myArray['vegetable'] = "carrot";
$myArray['color'] = "blue";

var_dump($myArray);
?>

array(3) {
  ["fruit"]=>
  string(5) "apple"
  ["vegetable"]=>
  string(6) "carrot"
  ["color"]=>
  string(4) "blue"
}
```

You can create arrays with multiple dimensions as well. You can think of this like a television show comprised of the title "Strangest Things" divided into seasons with individual episodes. As a variable in PHP, it could look like this:

```php
<?php
$strangestThings['season1']['episode1'] = "The Beginning";
//or
$strangestThings[0][0] = "The Beginning";
$strangestThings['season1']['episode3'] = "The Third Episode";

var_dump($strangestThings);
?>

array(2) {
  ["season1"]=>
  array(2) {
    ["episode1"]=>
    string(12) "The Beginning"
    ["episode3"]=>
    string(17) "The Third Episode"
  }
  [0]=>
  array(1) {
    [0]=>
    string(13) "The Beginning"
  }
}
```

Next, you'll explore the "object" in object-oriented programming.

Object

Objects as well as classes make up the main components of object-oriented programming (OOP). You can think of a class as the template or structure that an object will use when the new object is created and used. When an object datatype is created as a variable, let's say $myCar, it will have all of the properties and functionality of the $car class, including $model, $color, $price, and so on.

When the individual objects are created, they inherit all the properties and behaviors from the class, but each object will have different values for the properties.

Let's assume you have a class named Car. A Car can have properties like model and color. You can define variables like $model and $color to hold the values of these properties.

When the individual objects (Volvo, BMW, Toyota, etc.) are created, they inherit all the properties and behaviors from the class, but each object will have different values for the properties.

If you create a __construct() function, PHP will automatically call this function when you create an object from a class.

PHP Data Types: Special Types

In PHP, there are two special types:

- NULL
- Resource

NULL

NULL is a special value that represents a variable with no value. NULL is the only value that can possibly go in.

The special NULL value represents a variable with no value. NULL is the only possible value of a variable typed NULL to be considered null when

- The constant null has been assigned.

- There has been no other value set.

- It has been unset().

(chapter4-1.php)

```php
<?php
    $var = NULL;
    if(!isset($var)){
        echo 'Null value' ;
    }
?>

Null value
```

resource

Resources are not exactly a data type in PHP because they are mainly used to store some function calls or as references to external PHP resources.

Summary

In this chapter, you learned that in PHP there are different data types like scalar types (predefined), compound types (user-defined), and special types.

You also learned that PHP data types can be alphanumeric, whole numbers, floating points, and Boolean. You focused especially on strings, which are a very useful type in PHP and you will use them often. Remember that the power of strings comes in the many different manipulations that can be performed and the many different prebuilt string functions that are available.

In the next chapter, you will learn about PHP form data handling and you will see how to create and use forms to get form data using PHP superglobals such as $_GET and $_POST.

CHAPTER 5

Form Data

In this chapter, you will learn how to create and manage forms in PHP using the POST and GET methods.

You will explore three superglobals: $_POST, $_GET, and $_REQUEST. $_POST and $_GET are the two most common ways of receiving user input in PHP. $_REQUEST is lesser used.

This chapter consists of the following sections:

- PHP GET Form

- PHP POST Form

We once asked a junior developer to explain the difference between POST and GET (in general). The answer he gave, while less than ideal, was not incorrect. He said that POST is used to send data and GET is used to retrieve data. This is not wrong. When using a restful API, one would POST data to be used by the server and GET data as a request for a database query (for example). This, however, is not the answer we were expecting–or that he even knew he was talking about. The differences we were looking for between POST and GET are the following:

POST sends data via the HTTP body to an awaiting server (API, specific PHP file, etc..).

GET appends form data to the URL in a name-value pair.

The next time you hit the Submit button on a form, look at the URL. If you see any of the information you just filled out, then it is using GET. If the URL is clean, then surely POST is being used.

© Gunnard Engebreth, Satej Kumar Sahu 2023
G. Engebreth and S. K. Sahu, *PHP 8 Basics*, https://doi.org/10.1007/978-1-4842-8082-9_5

You don't even need to use a form to be using GET, to be honest. GET is a very useful way of persisting unique IDs, breadcrumbs, and miscellaneous data. They both have their function and use cases, but with both we need to keep security at the top. There was a TV show about a doctor who was famous for saying "Never trust a patient. They lie." In our case, NEVER trust user input. Exposing your code to an open attack vector like a form is just that... an attack vector. It is not a matter of "if" someone attempts to hack through the form but indeed 100% "when." If you look at your live server logs right now, you will see hundreds of requests coming in, scanning all files and directories that they can find. While they are attempting to find your exposed WordPress config file, they are also hitting the front end with bots to attempt SQL injections on your forms. Once you create a form, you have opened the door to the outside world and hackers will gladly walk in.

Now that I have scared you off completely from ever attempting to code again, this is manageable. There are tactics that can be employed that will slow down, deter, and even stop hackers from gaining access through code you have written. Having said all of that, THERE IS NO SUREFIRE WAY TO PROTECT AGAINST SQL INJECTIONS. There *are* many best practices that you can follow to feel as secure as possible, though, and you will learn about them after you get your own hacker red carpet, I mean form, set up.

PHP POST Form

Let's see how the PHP POST form works. Let's create a simple HTML form and see how $_POST receives data from the post request variable in the HTML page.

Here is a basic HTML form:

(basicForm.php)

```
<html>
<body>

<form action="functions.php" method="post">
Name: <input type="text" name="name"><br>
E-mail: <input type="text" name="email"><br>
<input type="submit">
</form>

</body>
</html>
```

This form takes the user input of name and email and sends them via POST to functions.php. The "method" is set by the method setting and where you are sending these values is set at the action setting. If you open up functions.php, you can see what happens next.

```
<?php
echo "Thank you {$_POST['name']}. I will email you at {$_
POST['email']}";
?>
<br />
<a href="basicForm.php">back</a>
```

This code takes (and assumes the validity of) the two POST variables sent from your form and prints them to the screen. You see name="name" and name="email" get sent over to functions.php and be retrieved with $_POST['name'] or $_POST['email']. If you change the name of email in the form page from name="email" to name="myEmail", then you would have to refer to it as $_POST['myEmail']. Let's try something real quick.

Instead of putting your name in the "name" field, try typing

```
<h1>pants</h1>
```

Now Press Enter and look at the results shown in Figure 5-1.

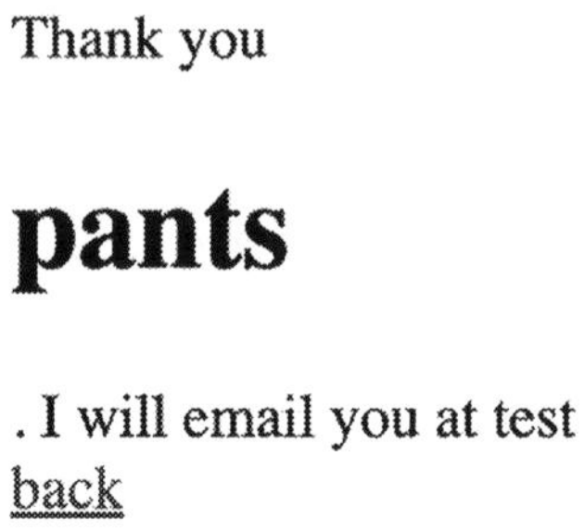

Thank you

pants

. I will email you at test
back

Figure 5-1. *Code result for the POST Form*

This is not the result the developer (you) were thinking about when creating this form. As a developer, you must always be thinking of not only the exact use case for your code; the fringe, edge cases, and worst cases must be considered. Users are very dependable and will consistently use applications the "right" way but there are cases in which the previous example can happen. Hopefully this happens because of a one-off mistype, but the reality is that more and more often attackers use forms like the one you built to utilize the lack of security measures to gain entrance into your system. Security must be at the forefront of a developer's mind, no matter where you work or how secure you think you may be.

Let's start to mitigate this situation.

Open up functions.php and add these lines to make the code look like this:

```php
<?php
$name = filter_var($_POST['name'], FILTER_SANITIZE_FULL_
SPECIAL_CHARS);
$email = filter_var($_POST['email'], FILTER_SANITIZE_EMAIL);
echo "Thank you {$name}. I will email you at {$email}";
?>
<br />
<a href="basicForm.php">back</a>
```

Go back and try to send <h1>pants</h1> as "name" again. You will see a different result this time. You are now blocking the HTML elements from being rendered by the browser. This is a positive step in the right direction. Many exploits that are live today begin with simple HTML elements rendering on a page. Now, let's see what you can do with the email address.

You are already sanitizing the email address to make sure that no sneaky characters get through, but you also want to validate that the address fits a certain format. You want to check if the email address they entered has a beginning part with letters and numbers and a few special characters like -. Then you want to check if there is an @ sign followed by more letters and numbers and then a period with a valid domain (.com, .org, .net, etc.). This can be done with the same filter_var function you used earlier but with the FILTER_VALIDATE_EMAIL option used. Open up functions.php again and add these lines of code to make it validate the email address:

```php
<?php
$emailErr= null;
$name = filter_var($_POST['name'], FILTER_SANITIZE_FULL_
SPECIAL_CHARS);
$email = filter_var($_POST['email'], FILTER_SANITIZE_EMAIL);
if (!filter_var($email, FILTER_VALIDATE_EMAIL)) {
  $emailErr = "Invalid email format";
}

if (!$emailErr) {
  echo "Thank you {$name}. I will email you at {$email}";
  } else {
        echo $emailErr;
}

?>
```

```
<br />
<a href="basicForm.php">back</a>
```

Reload the form and enter in a very non-email-addressy email like pants `one1@mail.$$$`.

This will return "Invalid email format" because it is an invalid email format (see how that works;) This method, of course, is not fool-proof. Without actually sending and receiving back a response from the email server from the domain that they have entered, you can't *actually* validate that this is a real and used email address. This is just to get you past the first check. Next would come a "Please check your email to validate you are a real user" step in order to make this more realistic.

Did you notice that after you received the "Invalid email format" message and clicked on the back button, your input was gone from the boxes? Your name and email were no longer there. Wouldn't it be nice if you included those things back in the box just in case someone mistyped a letter and didn't want to type everything again?

PHP GET Form

Let's see how the PHP GET form works.

You can do the above functionality easily with $_GET. Open up `functions.php` again and add these lines to the "back" link at the bottom:

```
<?php
$emailErr= null;
$name = filter_var($_POST['name'], FILTER_SANITIZE_FULL_
SPECIAL_CHARS);
$email = filter_var($_POST['email'], FILTER_SANITIZE_EMAIL);
if (!filter_var($email, FILTER_VALIDATE_EMAIL)) {
  $emailErr = "Invalid email format";
}
```

```
    if (!$emailErr) {
    echo "Thank you {$name}. I will email you at {$email}";
    } else {
            echo $emailErr;
    }

    ?>
<br />
<a href="basicForm.php?name=<?= $name ?>&email=<?=
$email?>">back</a>
```

Here you are adding the $name and $email variables to the URL so that you can use them when you get back to shortForm.php. What is with <?=, though? This is how you can use PHO with its short open option. Instead of typing <?php when you want to use PHP code within HTML to do something simple, you can use the short open <?= and the = means echo. So, with this in your toolbox, you can quickly put the $name and $email variables where you need to in the URL to use the $_GET variable back on the basicForm.php page. Go ahead and open that file up, too, and add these lines:

```
<?php
if (isset($_GET)) {
        if (isset($_GET['name'])) {
                $name = $_GET['name'];
        }
        if (isset($_GET['email'])) {
                $email = $_GET['email'];
        }
}

$name != '' ? $name : '';
$email != '' ? $email : '';
?>
```

```
<html>
<body>
<form action="functions.php" method="post">
Name: <input type="text" name="name" value="<?= $name; ?>"><br>
E-mail: <input type="text" name="email" value="<?= $email;
?>"><br>
<input type="submit">
</form>
</body>
</html>
```

The form page will now check to see if there are any variables set within the $_GET super global. If there are, it checks if $_GET['name'] and $_GET['email'] are set. If there is anything in there, it sets them to $name and $email, respectively. Next, it checks if $name or $email have been set or not. This is a ternary if statement. Instead of typing

```
if ($name != "" ) {
        $name = $name;
} else {
        $name = "";
}
```

you can just say

```
(Conditional statement) ? (Statement_1) : (Statement_2);
```

So, what you want is

```
$name != "" ? $name : ""
```

If $name is not empty, then set it to $name otherwise set it to "".

In the input box you use the value setting to add the name or email you just received (or not) from $_GET via the URL. Now that you can get user information and pass it back to your own scripts, you can fully interact with users. Using the $_GET and $_POST superglobals gets you familiar with arrays, specifically associative arrays.

Summary

In this chapter, you learned about PHP form data handling. You learned how to create and use forms to get form data using PHP superglobals such as $_GET and $_POST.

In the next chapter, you will learn more and take a deeper look into arrays, which are used to hold in a single variable multiple values of a similar type.

CHAPTER 6

Arrays

In the previous chapters, you learned how to deal with PHP variables. In this chapter, we will teach you how to create and manage PHP arrays.

Say you need to hold multiple values of a similar type in a single variable, without creating additional variables to store those values. How would you do this? By using PHP arrays.

This chapter consists of the following sections:

- PHP Indexed and Associative Arrays

- PHP Multidimensional Arrays

- PHP Array Functions

PHP Indexed and Associative Arrays

Arrays are one of the most versatile and useful elements in PHP. Just what is an array? Arrays are used to store multiple values within a single variable. Think of an array as a container with multiple sections. With this container, you can store and organize other information, including variables.

With PHP associative arrays, you can associate a name with each array element in PHP just by using the => symbol.

This can look like

```
array(
    key  => value,
    key2 => value2,
    key3 => value3,
    ...
)
```

With a PHP indexed array, a PHP index is represented by a number, starting from 0, like this:

```
$city=array("Rome","Naples","Milan");

$city[0] = "Rome";
$city[1] = "Naples";
$city[3] = "Milan";
```

Actual PHP code with an associative array looks like the following:
Chapter6/firstArray.php

```
<?php

$array1 = array(
    "foo" => "bar",
    "bar" => "foo",
);

// Using the short array syntax
$array2 = [
    "foo2" => "bar2",
    "bar2" => "foo2",
];

var_dump($array1);
echo '<br />';
var_dump($array2);
```

The output looks like this:

```
array(2) { ["foo"]=> string(3) "bar" ["bar"]=>
string(3) "foo" }
array(2) { ["foo2"]=> string(4) "bar2" ["bar2"]=> string(4)
"foo2" }
```

The first part, array(2), tells you that the variable you are using, var_dump, is of type array. The 2 indicates how many elements are held within this array. The next part is the key=>value pair listing. The key is in the square brackets and the value is to the right of the => sign. Looking to the direct right of => you see string(3), which tells you that the value in the key=>value pair is a string with a length of 3 ("bar"). Let's look at firstArray2.php to see some examples using different types of variables.

```php
<?php
$array = array(
    "foo" => "bar",
    "bar" => "foo",
    100   => -100,
    -100  => 100,
);
var_dump($array);
?>
```

Here the output is

```
array(4) { ["foo"]=> string(3) "bar" ["bar"]=> string(3) "foo"
[100]=> int(-100) [-100]=> int(100) }
```

Notice you have data of types string and int within this array. So far you have used the key=>value relationship to define your arrays, but what if you don't "need" a key? For example, what if you are just using the array to store the first names of preferred customers. You would not want to use

```
"Customer" => "john",
"Customer" => "peter",
etc...
```

This would not work. First, you can't successfully use the same key for multiple values. And second, it is just useless. PHP automatically assigns a numeric key when one is not defined by the user.

firstArray3.php

```php
<?php
$array = array("foo", "bar", "hello", "world");
var_dump($array);
```

The output is

```
array(4) { [0]=> string(3) "foo" [1]=> string(3) "bar" [2]=>
string(5) "hello" [3]=> string(5) "world" }
```

You can see that instead of a key that you defined, PHP uses numbers in its place. Notice that the array starts at 0 instead of 1. With all the many programming languages and their differences, they all agree on one thing: arrays start at 0.

If you have been following along so far, you may be wondering if you can have an array WITHIN an array. The answer is yes. They are called multidimensional arrays. Take a look at firstArray4.php.

```php
<?php
$array = array(
    "foo" => "bar",
    42     => 24,
    "multi" => array(
        "dimensional" => array(
            "array" => "foobar"
        )
    )
);
```

```php
var_dump($array["foo"]);
var_dump($array[42]);
var_dump($array["multi"]["dimensional"]["array"]);
```

The output is

```
string(3) "bar" int(42) string(6) "foobar"
```

The first two examples,

```php
var_dump($array["foo"]);
var_dump($array[42]);
```

are pretty straightforward but the last one,

```php
var_dump($array["multi"]["dimensional"]["array"]);
```

is more complicated and needs a bit of explaining. This is the multidimensional array. Think of it like a song on an album. You might refer to this specific song while talking to your friend as $artist['album']['trackNumber']. Or if the artist has a large catalog of music, then it could be $music['artist']['album']['trackNumber'] and $music['elvis']['live'][1] would be the first song on Elvis' album named "Live." Things can get pretty hairy with multidimensional arrays but sometimes they are the only way to store and organize the data you are using.

Here are some more use cases for multidimensional arrays:
multiArray1.php

```php
<?php
$cars = array (
  array("Subaru",21,17),
  array("Toyota",13,12),
  array("Lexus",6,8),
  array("Ford",14,10)
);
```

Here you see that you can create a two-dimensional array using data from a used car lot. You are keeping track of the car brand, units available, and units sold. Your main array contains four separate arrays with the specific data. Cars is an array with the first element being an array containing Subaru, 21, and 17. To access Subaru, you use

```
$cars[0][0];
```

This means, within the $cars array, you want the first ([0]) element of the first ([0]) element. If you want to access 21, you use $cars[0][1], meaning you want the second element ([1]) of the first ([0]) element.

```
echo $cars[0][0] . ": In available: " . $cars[0][1] . ", sold:
" . $cars[0][2] . " " . <br>";
echo $cars[1][0] . ": In available: " . $cars[1][1] . ", sold:
" . $cars[1][2] . " " . <br>";
echo $cars[2][0] . ": In available: " . $cars[2][1] . ", sold:
" . $cars[2][2] . " " . <br>";
echo $cars[3][0] . ": In available: " . $cars[3][1] . ", sold:
" . $cars[3][2] . " " . <br>";
```

Whenever you need to work through data that is stored in an array, for loops are a great solution. Here you iterate through the array and print out the needed information:

```
for ($row = 0; $row < 4; $row++) {
  echo "<p><b>Row #$row -- {$cars[$row][0]}</b></p>";
  echo "<ul>";
  for ($col = 1; $col < 3; $col++) {
    echo "<li>".$cars[$row][$col]."</li>";
  }
  echo "</ul>";
}
```

PHP Multidimensional Arrays

A PHP multidimensional array is also known as an array of arrays, and it is generally used when you need to store, for instance, tabular data in an array and provide it in a matrix of row * column.

A multidimensional array looks like this:

```
Definition
$emp = array
  (
  array(1,"Luna",10000),
  array(2,"Leo",20000),
  array(3,"Neve",30000)
  );
```

PHP Array Functions

You've now learned about indexed, associative, and multidimensional arrays, so let's move onto PHP array functions, which are used in the PHP language to access and manipulate the elements of an array.

The PHP array's built-in functions are generally used when you need to create a simple and multi-dimensional array.

Here is the full list of the PHP array functions; they will explained in this chapter.

array_chunk()	array_rand()	current()
array_combine()	array_reduce()	end()
array_count_values()	array_replace_recursive()	extract()
array_diff_assoc()	array_replace()	in_array()
array_diff_keys()	array_reverse()	key()
array_diff_uassoc()	array_search()	krsort()
array_diff_ukey()	array_shift()	ksort()
array_diff()	array_slice()	list()
array_fill_keys()	array_splice()	natcasesort()
array_fill()	array_sum()	natsort()
array_filter()	array_udiff_assoc()	next()
array_flip()	array_udiff()	pos()
array_intersect_assoc()	array_uintersect_assoc()	prev()
array_intersect_key()	array_uintersect_uassoc()	range()
	array_uintersect()	reset()
array_intersect_uassoc()	array_unique()	rsort()
array_intersect()	array_unshift()	shuffle()
array_key_exists()	array_values()	sizeof()
array_keys()	array_walk_recursive()	sort()
array_merge_recursive()	array_walk()	uasort()
	array()	uksort()
array_multisort()	arsort()	usort()
array_pad()	asort()	each()
array_pop()	compact()	
array_product()	count()	
array_push()		

Let's now introduce some of the most used and common PHP Array functions.

array_change_key_case

Changes the case of all keys in an array

```
array_change_key_case(array $array, int $case = CASE_
LOWER): array
```

Returns an array with all keys from the array lowercased or uppercased. Numbered indices are left as is.

Parameters

array

The array to work on

case

Either CASE_UPPER or CASE_LOWER (default)

Return values

Returns an array with its keys lowercased or uppercased, or null if the array is not an array

array_chunk

Splits an array into chunks

```
array_chunk(array $array, int $length, bool $preserve_keys =
false): array
```

Chunks an array into arrays with length elements. The last chunk may contain less than the length elements.

Parameters

array

The array to work on

length

The size of each chunk

preserve_keys

When set to true, keys will be preserved. The default is false, which will reindex the chunk numerically.

Return values

Returns a multidimensional numerically indexed array, starting with 0, with each dimension containing length elements

array_column

Returns the values from a single column in the input array

```
array_column(array $array, int|string|null $column_key,
int|string|null $index_key = null): array
```

array_column() returns the values from a single column of the array, identified by the column_key. Optionally, an index_key may be provided to index the values in the returned array by the values from the index_key column of the input array.

Parameters

array

A multi-dimensional array or an array of objects from which to pull a column of values. If an array of objects is provided, then public properties can be directly pulled. In order for protected or private properties to be pulled, the class must implement both the __get() and __isset() magic methods.

column_key

The column of values to return. This value may be an integer key of the column you wish to retrieve, or it may be a string key name for an associative array or property name. It may also be null to return complete arrays or objects (this is useful together with index_key to reindex the array).

index_key

The column to use as the index/key for the returned array. This value may be the integer key of the column or it may be the string key name. The value is cast as usual for array keys (however, prior to PHP 8.0.0, objects supporting conversion to string were also allowed).

Return values

Returns an array of values representing a single column from the input array

array_combine

Creates an array by using the values from the keys array as keys and the values from the values array as the corresponding values

```
array_combine(array $keys, array $values): array
```

Parameters

keys

Array of keys to be used. Illegal values for a key will be converted to a string.

values

Array of values to be used

Return values

Returns the combined array or false if the number of elements for each array isn't equal

array_count_values

array_count_values() returns an array using the values of array as keys and their frequency in array as values.

```
array_count_values(array $array): array
```

Parameters

array

The array of values to count

Return values

Returns an associative array of values from an array as keys and their count as value

array_diff_assoc

Computes the difference of the arrays with an additional index check

```
array_diff_assoc(array $array, array ...$arrays): array
```

Unlike `array_diff()`, the array keys are also used in the comparison.

Parameters

array

The array to compare from

arrays

Arrays to compare against

Return values

Returns an array containing all the values from the array that are not present in any of the other arrays

array_diff_key

Computes the difference of arrays using keys for comparison

```
array_diff_key(array $array, array ...$arrays): array
```

This function is like `array_diff()` except the comparison is done on the keys instead of the values.

Parameters

array

The array to compare from

arrays

Arrays to compare against

Return values

Returns an array containing all the entries from the array whose keys are absent from all of the other arrays

array_diff_uassoc

Computes the difference of the arrays with an additional index check, which is performed by a user-supplied callback function. Unlike `array_diff()`, the array keys are used in the comparison.

`array_diff_uassoc(array $array, array ...$arrays, callable $key_compare_func): array`

Unlike `array_diff_assoc()`, a user-supplied callback function is used for the indices comparison, not an internal function.

Parameters

array

The array to compare from

arrays

Arrays to compare against

key_compare_func

The comparison function must return an integer less than, equal to, or greater than zero if the first argument is considered to be respectively less than, equal to, or greater than the second.

`callback(mixed $a, mixed $b): int`

Return values

Returns an array containing all the entries from the array that are not present in any of the other arrays

array_diff_ukey

Compares the keys from the array against the keys from arrays and returns the difference. This function is like `array_diff()`, except the comparison is done on the keys instead of the values.

```
array_diff_ukey(array $array, array ...$arrays, callable $key_
compare_func): array
```

Unlike `array_diff_key()`, a user-supplied callback function is used for the indices comparison, not an internal function.

Parameters

array

The array to compare from

arrays

Arrays to compare against

key_compare_func

The comparison function must return an integer less than, equal to, or greater than zero if the first argument is considered to be respectively less than, equal to, or greater than the second.

```
callback(mixed $a, mixed $b): int
```

Return values

Returns an array containing all the entries from the array that are not present in any of the other arrays

array_diff

Computes the difference of arrays

```
array_diff(array $array, array ...$arrays): array
```

Compares an array against one or more other arrays and returns the values in the array that are not present in any of the other arrays

Parameters

array

The array to compare from

arrays

Arrays to compare against

Return values

Returns an array containing all the entries from the array that are not present in any of the other arrays. Keys in the array are preserved.

array_fill_keys

Fills an array with the value of the value parameter, using the values of the keys array as keys

```
array_fill_keys(array $keys, mixed $value): array
```

Parameters

keys

Array of values that will be used as keys. Illegal values for a key will be converted to a string.

value

Value to use for filling

Return values

Returns the filled array

array_fill

Fills an array with values

```
array_fill(int $start_index, int $count, mixed $value): array
```

Fills an array with count entries of the value of the value parameter, with keys starting at the start_index parameter

Parameters

start_index

The first index of the returned array. If start_index is negative, the first index of the returned array will be start_index and the following indices will start from 0 (see example).

count

Number of elements to insert. Must be greater than or equal to zero.

value

Value to use for filling

Return values

Returns the filled array

array_filter

Filters elements of an array using a `callback` function

```
array_filter(array $array, ?callable $callback = null, int
$mode = 0): array
```

Iterates over each value in the array, passing them to the `callback` function. If the `callback` function returns true, the current value from the array is returned into the result array.

Array keys are preserved and may result in gaps if the array was indexed. The result array can be reindexed using the `array_values()` function.

Parameters

array

The array to iterate over

callback

The callback function to use. If no callback is supplied, all empty entries of `array` will be removed. See `empty()` for how PHP defines empty in this case.

mode

Flag determining what arguments are sent to `callback`:

ARRAY_FILTER_USE_KEY

Passes the key as the only argument to `callback` instead of the value

ARRAY_FILTER_USE_BOTH

Passes both value and key as arguments to `callback` instead of the value. Default is 0, which will pass value as the only argument to callback instead.

Return values

Returns the filtered array

array_flip

Exchanges all keys with their associated values in an array

```
array_flip(array $array): array
```

`array_flip()` returns an array in flip order; in other words, keys from the array become values and values from the array become keys.

Note that the values of array need to be valid keys, so they need to be either an int or a string. You will get a warning if a value has the wrong type, and the key/value pair in question will not be included in the result.

If a value has several occurrences, the latest key will be used as its value, and all others will be lost.

Parameters

array

An array of key/value pairs to be flipped

Return values

Returns the flipped array

array_intersect_assoc

Computes the intersection of arrays with an additional index check

```
array_intersect_assoc(array $array, array ...$arrays): array
```

array_intersect_assoc() returns an array containing all the values of an array that are present in all the arguments. Note that the keys are also used in the comparison, unlike in array_intersect().

Parameters

array

The array with master values to check

arrays

Arrays to compare values against

Return values

Returns an associative array containing all the values in the array that are present in all of the arguments

array_intersect_key

Computes the intersection of arrays using keys for comparison

array_intersect_key(array $array, array ...$arrays): array

array_intersect_key() returns an array containing all the entries of an array that have keys that are present in all the arguments.

Parameters

array

The array with master keys to check

arrays

Arrays to compare keys against

Return values

Returns an associative array containing all the entries of the array that have keys that are present in all arguments

array_intersect_uassoc

Computes the intersection of arrays with an additional index check and compares indexes by a callback function

```
array_intersect_uassoc(array $array, array ...$arrays, callable
$key_compare_func): array
```

array_intersect_uassoc() returns an array containing all the values of array that are present in all the arguments. Note that the keys are used in the comparison, unlike in array_intersect().

Parameters

array

Initial array for the comparison of the arrays

arrays

Arrays to compare keys against

key_compare_func

The comparison function must return an integer less than, equal to, or greater than zero if the first argument is considered to be respectively less than, equal to, or greater than the second.

```
callback(mixed $a, mixed $b): int
```

Return values

Returns the values of array whose values exist in all of the arguments

array_intersect_ukey

Computes the intersection of arrays using a callback function on the keys for comparison

```
array_intersect_ukey(array $array, array ...$arrays, callable
$key_compare_func): array
```

array_intersect_ukey() returns an array containing all the values of an array that have matching keys that are present in all the arguments.

Parameters

array

Initial array for comparison of the arrays

```
arrays
```
Arrays to compare keys against
```
key_compare_func
```
The comparison function must return an integer less than, equal to, or greater than zero if the first argument is considered to be respectively less than, equal to, or greater than the second.

```
callback(mixed $a, mixed $b): int
```

Return values

Returns the values of array whose keys exist in all the arguments

array_intersect

Computes the intersection of arrays

```
array_intersect(array $array, array ...$arrays): array
```

`array_intersect()` returns an array containing all the values of an array that are present in all the arguments. Note that keys are preserved.

Parameters

```
array
```
The array with master values to check
```
arrays
```
Arrays to compare values against

Return values

Returns an array containing all of the values in the array whose values exist in all of the parameters

array_is_list

Checks whether a given array is a list

```
array_is_list(array $array): bool
```

An array is considered a list if its keys consist of consecutive numbers from 0 to count($array)-1.

Parameters

array

The array being evaluated

Return values

Returns true if array is a list or false otherwise

array_key_exists

Checks if the given key or index exists in the array

```
array_key_exists(string|int $key, array $array): bool
```

array_key_exists() returns true if the given key is set in the array. A key can be any value possible for an array index.

Parameters

key

Value to check

array

An array with keys to check

Return values

Returns true on success or false on failure

array_key_first

Gets the first key of an array without affecting the internal array pointer

```
array_key_first(array $array): int|string|null
```

Parameters

array

An array

Return values

Returns the first key of array if the array is not empty or null otherwise

array_key_last

Gets the last key of an array without affecting the internal array pointer

```
array_key_last(array $array): int|string|null
```

Parameters

array

An array

Return values

Returns the last key of array if the array is not empty or null otherwise

array_keys

Returns all the keys or a subset of the keys of an array

```
array_keys(array $array): array
array_keys(array $array, mixed $search_value, bool $strict =
false): array
```

array_keys() returns the keys, numeric and string, from the array. If a search_value is specified, then only the keys for that value are returned. Otherwise, all the keys from the array are returned.

Parameters

array

An array containing keys to return

search_value

If specified, then only keys containing this value are returned.

strict

Determines if the strict comparison (===) should be used during the search.

Return values

Returns an array of all the keys in array

array_map

Applies the callback to the elements of the given arrays

```
array_map(?callable $callback, array $array, array
...$arrays): array
```

array_map() returns an array containing the results of applying the callback to the corresponding value of the array (and arrays if more arrays are provided) used as arguments for the callback. The number of parameters that the callback function accepts should match the number of arrays passed to array_map(). Excess input arrays are ignored. An ArgumentCountError is thrown if an insufficient number of arguments is provided.

Parameters

callback

A callable to run for each element in each array. Null can be passed as a value to callback to perform a zip operation on multiple arrays. If only an array is provided, array_map() will return the input array.

array

An array to run through the callback function

arrays

Supplementary variable list of array arguments to run through the callback function

Return values

Returns an array containing the results of applying the callback function to the corresponding value of the array (and arrays if more arrays are provided) used as arguments for the callback

The returned array will preserve the keys of the array argument if and only if exactly one array is passed. If more than one array is passed, the returned array will have sequential integer keys.

array_merge_recursive

Merges one or more arrays recursively

```
array_merge_recursive(array ...$arrays): array
```

array_merge_recursive() merges the elements of one or more arrays together so that the values of one are appended to the end of the previous one. It returns the resulting array.

If the input arrays have the same string keys, then the values for these keys are merged together into an array, and this is done recursively, so that if one of the values is an array itself, the function will merge it with a corresponding entry in another array too. If, however, the arrays have the same numeric key, the later value will not overwrite the original value, but will be appended.

Parameters

arrays

Variable list of arrays to recursively merge

Return values

An array of values resulted from merging the arguments together. If called without any arguments, it returns an empty array.

array_merge

Merges one or more arrays

```
array_merge(array ...$arrays): array
```

Merges the elements of one or more arrays together so that the values of one are appended to the end of the previous one. It returns the resulting array.

If the input arrays have the same string keys, the later value for that key will overwrite the previous one. If the arrays contain numeric keys, the later value will not overwrite the original value but will be appended.

108

Values in the input arrays with numeric keys will be renumbered with incrementing keys starting from zero in the result array.

Parameters

arrays

Variable list of arrays to merge

Return values

Returns the resulting array. If called without any arguments, returns an empty array.

array_multisort

Sorts multiple or multi-dimensional arrays

array1_sort_flags

Sorts options for the previous array argument

Sorting type flags:

SORT_REGULAR compares items normally (doesn't change types).

SORT_NUMERIC compares items numerically.

SORT_STRING compares items as strings.

SORT_LOCALE_STRING compares items as strings, based on the current locale. It uses the locale, which can be changed using setlocale().

SORT_NATURAL compares items as strings using "natural ordering" like natsort().

SORT_FLAG_CASE can be combined (bitwise OR) with SORT_STRING or SORT_NATURAL to sort strings case-insensitively.

This argument can be swapped with array1_sort_order or omitted entirely, in which case SORT_REGULAR is assumed.

rest

More arrays, optionally followed by sort order and flags. Only elements corresponding to equivalent elements in previous arrays are compared. In other words, the sort is lexicographical.

Return values

Returns true on success or false on failure

array_pad

Pada an array to the specified length with a value

```
array_pad(array $array, int $length, mixed $value): array
```

array_pad() returns a copy of the array padded to a size specified by length with the value value. If length is positive, then the array is padded on the right; if it's negative, then on the left. If the absolute value of the length is less than or equal to the length of the array, then no padding takes place. It is possible to add at most 1,048,576 elements at a time.

Parameters

array

Initial array of values to pad

length

New size of the array

value

Value to pad if array is less than length

Return values

Returns a copy of the array padded to size specified by length with the value value. If the length is positive, then the array is padded on the right; if it's negative, then it's on the left. If the absolute value of length is less than or equal to the length of the array, then no padding takes place.

array_pop

Pops the element off the end of array

```
array_pop(array &$array): mixed
```

```
array_pop()
```

Note   This function will reset() the array pointer of the input array after use.

Parameters

array

The array to get the value from

Return values

Returns the value of the last element of array. If the array is empty (or is not an array), null will be returned.

array_product

Calculates the product of values in an array

```
array_product(array $array): int|float
```

Parameters

array

The array

Return values

Returns the product as an integer or float

array_push

Pushes one or more elements onto the end of array

```
array_push(array &$array, mixed ...$values): int
```

array_push() treats an array as a stack and pushes the passed-in variables onto the end of array. The length of the array increases by the number of variables pushed. This has the same effect as

```php
<?php
$array[] = $var;
?>
```

repeated for each passed value.

If you use `array_push()` to add one element to the array, it's better to use `$array[]` = because in that way there is no overhead of calling a function.

Parameters

array

The input array

values

The values to push onto the end of the array

Return values

Returns the new number of elements in the array

array_rand

Picks one or more random keys out of an array returns the key (or keys) of the random entries.

```
array_rand(array $array, int $num = 1): int|string|array
```

It uses a pseudo random number generator that is not suitable for cryptographic purposes.

Parameters

array

The input array

num

Specifies how many entries should be picked

Return values

When picking only one entry, `array_rand()` returns the key for a random entry. Otherwise, an array of keys for the random entries is returned. This is done so that random keys can be picked from the array as well as random values. If multiple keys are returned, they will be returned in the order they were present in the original array. Trying to pick more elements than there are in the array will result in an `E_WARNING` level error and NULL will be returned.

array_reduce

Iteratively reduces the array to a single value using a `callback` function

```
array_reduce(array $array, callable $callback, mixed
$initial = null): mixed
```

Parameters

array

The input array

callback

callback(mixed $carry, mixed $item): mixed

carry

Holds the return value of the previous iteration; in the case of the first iteration, it instead holds the value of `initial`.

item

Holds the value of the current iteration

initial

If the optional `initial` is available, it will be used at the beginning of the process, or as a final result in case the array is empty.

Return values

Returns the resulting value. If the array is empty and `initial` is not passed, `array_reduce()` returns null.

array_replace_recursive

Replaces elements from passed arrays into the first array recursively

```
array_replace_recursive(array $array, array
...$replacements): array
```

`array_replace_recursive()` replaces the values of array with the same values from all the following arrays. If a key from the first array exists in the second array, its value will be replaced by the value from the second array. If the key exists in the second array, and not the first, it will be created in the first array. If a key only exists in the first array, it will be left as is. If several arrays are passed for replacement, they will be processed in order, the later array overwriting the previous values.

array_replace_recursive() is recursive: it will recurse into arrays and apply the same process to the inner value.

When the value in the first array is scalar, it will be replaced by the value in the second array, whether its scalar or array. When the value in the first array and the second array are both arrays, array_replace_recursive() will replace their respective value recursively.

Parameters

array

The array in which elements are replaced

replacements

Arrays from which elements will be extracted

Return values

Returns an array or null if an error occurs

array_replace

Replaces elements from passed arrays into the first array

```
array_replace(array $array, array ...$replacements): array
```

array_replace() replaces the values of array with values having the same keys in each of the following arrays. If a key from the first array exists in the second array, its value will be replaced by the value from the second array. If the key exists in the second array, and not the first, it will be created in the first array. If a key only exists in the first array, it will be left as is. If several arrays are passed for replacement, they will be processed in order, the later arrays overwriting the previous values.

array_replace() is not recursive: it will replace values in the first array by whatever type is in the second array.

Parameters

array

The array in which elements are replaced

replacements

Arrays from which elements will be extracted. Values from later arrays overwrite the previous values.

Return values

Returns an array or null if an error occurs

array_reverse

Return an array with elements in reverse order

```
array_reverse(array $array, bool $preserve_keys = false): array
```

Parameters

array

The input array

preserve_keys

If set to true, numeric keys are preserved. Non-numeric keys are not affected by this setting and will always be preserved.

Return values

Returns the reversed array

array_search

Searches the array for a given value and returns the first corresponding key if successful

```
array_search(mixed $needle, array $haystack, bool $strict =
false): int|string|false
```

Searches for needle in haystack

Parameters

needle

The searched value

Note If the needle is a string, the comparison is done in a case-sensitive manner.

---

haystack

The array

strict

If the third parameter, strict, is set to true, the array_search() function will search for identical elements in the haystack. This means it will also perform a strict type comparison of the needle in the haystack, and objects must be the same instance.

Return values

Returns the key for needle if it is found in the array and false otherwise

If needle is found in haystack more than once, the first matching key is returned. To return the keys for all matching values, use array_keys() with the optional search_value parameter instead.

array_shift

Shifts an element off the beginning of array

array_shift(array &$array): mixed

array_shift() shifts the first value of the array off and returns it, shortening the array by one element and moving everything down. All numerical array keys will be modified to start counting from 0 while literal keys won't be affected.

Parameters

array

The input array

Return values

Returns the shifted value or null if array is empty or is not an array

array_slice

Extracts a slice of the array

```
array_slice(
    array $array,
    int $offset,
    ?int $length = null,
    bool $preserve_keys = false
): array
```

array_slice() returns the sequence of elements from the array array as specified by the offset and length parameters.

Parameters

array

The input array

offset

If offset is non-negative, the sequence will start at that offset in the array.

If offset is negative, the sequence will start that far from the end of the array.

Note   The offset parameter denotes the position in the array, not the key.

---

length

If length is given and is positive, the sequence will have up to that many elements in it.

117

If the array is shorter than the length, only the available array elements will be present.

If length is given and is negative, the sequence will stop that many elements from the end of the array.

If it is omitted, the sequence will have everything from offset up until the end of the array.

preserve_keys

Note   array_slice() will reorder and reset the integer array indices by default. This behavior can be changed by setting preserve_keys to true. String keys are always preserved, regardless of this parameter.

Return values

Returns the slice. If the offset is larger than the size of the array, an empty array is returned.

array_splice

Removes a portion of the array and replaces it with something else

```
array_splice(
    array &$array,
    int $offset,
    ?int $length = null,
    mixed $replacement = []
): array
```

Removes the elements designated by offset and length from the array array and replaces them with the elements of the replacement array, if supplied.

Parameters

array

The input array

offset

If offset is positive, then the start of the removed portion is at that offset from the beginning of the array array.

If offset is negative, then the start of the removed portion is at that offset from the end of the array array.

length

If length is omitted, remove everything from offset to the end of the array.

If length is specified and is positive, that many elements will be removed.

If length is specified and is negative, the end of the removed portion will be that many elements from the end of the array.

If length is specified and is 0, no elements will be removed.

Tip   To remove everything from offset to the end of the array when replacement is also specified, use count($input) for length.

---

replacement

If a replacement array is specified, then the removed elements are replaced with elements from this array.

If offset and length are such that nothing is removed, the elements from the replacement array are inserted in the place specified by the offset.

If replacement is just one element, it is not necessary to put array() or square brackets around it, unless the element is an array itself, an object or null.

Return values

Returns an array consisting of the extracted elements

array_sum

Calculates the sum of values in an array

```
array_sum(array $array): int|float
```

Parameters

array

The input array

Return values

Returns the sum of values as an integer or float, or 0 if the array is empty

array_udiff_assoc

Computes the difference of arrays with an additional index check and compares data by a `callback` function

```
array_udiff_assoc(array $array, array ...$arrays, callable $value_compare_func): array
```

Parameters

array

The first array

arrays

Arrays to compare against

value_compare_func

The comparison function must return an integer less than, equal to, or greater than zero if the first argument is considered to be respectively less than, equal to, or greater than the second.

```
callback(mixed $a, mixed $b): int
```

Return values

`array_udiff_assoc()` returns an array containing all the values from the array that are not present in any of the other arguments. Note that the keys are used in the comparison, unlike `array_diff()` and `array_udiff()`. The comparison of the arrays' data is performed by using a user-supplied callback. In this aspect, the behavior is opposite the behavior of `array_diff_assoc()`, which uses an internal function for comparison.

array_udiff_uassoc

Computes the difference of arrays with an additional index check and compares data and indexes by a callback function

```
array_udiff_uassoc(
    array $array,
    array ...$arrays,
    callable $value_compare_func,
    callable $key_compare_func
): array
```

Note that the keys are used in the comparison, unlike `array_diff()` and `array_udiff()`.

Parameters

array

The first array

arrays

Arrays to compare against

value_compare_func

The comparison function must return an integer less than, equal to, or greater than zero if the first argument is considered to be respectively less than, equal to, or greater than the second.

`callback(mixed $a, mixed $b): int`

key_compare_func

The comparison of keys (indices) is done also by the callback function `key_compare_func`. This behavior is unlike what `array_udiff_assoc()` does, since the latter compares the indices by using an internal function.

Return values

Returns an array containing all the values from array that are not present in any of the other arguments

array_udiff

Computes the difference of arrays by using a callback function for data comparison

```
array_udiff(array $array, array ...$arrays, callable $value_
compare_func): array
```

This is unlike `array_diff()`, which uses an internal function for comparing the data.

Parameters

array

The first array

arrays

Arrays to compare against

value_compare_func

The callback comparison function. The comparison function must return an integer less than, equal to, or greater than zero if the first argument is considered to be respectively less than, equal to, or greater than the second.

```
callback(mixed $a, mixed $b): int
```

Return values

Returns an array containing all the values of array that are not present in any of the other arguments

array_uintersect_assoc

Computes the intersection of arrays with an additional index check and compares data by a callback function

```
array_uintersect_assoc(array $array, array ...$arrays, callable
$value_compare_func): array
```

Note that the keys are used in the comparison, unlike in `array_uintersect()`. The data is compared by using a callback function.

Parameters

array

The first array

arrays

Arrays to compare against

value_compare_func

The comparison function must return an integer less than, equal to, or greater than zero if the first argument is considered to be respectively less than, equal to, or greater than the second.

```
callback(mixed $a, mixed $b): int
```

Return values

Returns an array containing all the values of array that are present in all the arguments

array_uintersect_uassoc

Computes the intersection of arrays with an additional index check and compares data and indexes by separate callback functions

```
array_uintersect_uassoc(
    array $array1,
    array ...$arrays,
```

```
    callable $value_compare_func,
    callable $key_compare_func
): array
```

Parameters

> array1
> The first array
> arrays
> Further arrays
> value_compare_func

The comparison function must return an integer less than, equal to, or greater than zero if the first argument is considered to be respectively less than, equal to, or greater than the second.

```
callback(mixed $a, mixed $b): int
```

> key_compare_func
> Key comparison callback function

Return values

> Returns an array containing all the values of array1 that are present in all the arguments

array_uintersect

Computes the intersection of arrays and compares data by a callback function

```
array_uintersect(array $array, array ...$arrays, callable
$value_compare_func): array
```

Parameters

> array
> The first array
> arrays

Arrays to compare against

value_compare_func

The comparison function must return an integer less than, equal to, or greater than zero if the first argument is considered to be respectively less than, equal to, or greater than the second.

```
callback(mixed $a, mixed $b): int
```

Return values

Returns an array containing all the values of array that are present in all the arguments

array_unique

Removes duplicate values from an array

```
array_unique(array $array, int $flags = SORT_STRING): array
```

It takes an input array and returns a new array without duplicate values.

Note that keys are preserved. If multiple elements compare equally under the given flags, then the key and value of the first equal element will be retained.

Note   Two elements are considered equal if and only if (string) $elem1 === (string) $elem2; in other words, when the string representation is the same, the first element will be used.

Parameters

array

The input array

flags

The optional second parameter of `flags` may be used to modify the sorting behavior using these values:

Sorting type flags:

`SORT_REGULAR` compares items normally (doesn't change types).

`SORT_NUMERIC` compares items numerically.

`SORT_STRING` compares items as strings.

`SORT_LOCALE_STRING` compares items as strings, based on the current locale.

Return values

Returns the filtered array

array_unshift

Prepends one or more elements to the beginning of an array

```
array_unshift(array &$array, mixed ...$values): int
```

Note that the list of elements is prepended as a whole, so that the prepended elements stay in the same order. All numerical array keys will be modified to start counting from zero while literal keys won't be changed.

Parameters

`array`

The input array

`values`

The values to prepend

Return values

Returns the new number of elements in the array

array_values

Returns all the values of an array and indexes the array numerically

```
array_values(array $array): array
```

Parameters

array

The array

Return values

Returns an indexed array of values

array_walk_recursive

Applies a user function recursively to every member of an array

```
array_walk_recursive(array|object &$array, callable $callback,
mixed $arg = null): bool
```

This function will recurse into deeper arrays.

Parameters

array

The input array

callback

Typically, callback takes on two parameters, the array parameter's value and the key/index.

arg

If the optional arg parameter is supplied, it will be passed as the third parameter to the callback.

Return values

Returns true on success or false on failure

array_walk

Applies a user-supplied function to every member of an array

```
array_walk(array|object &$array, callable $callback, mixed $arg
= null): bool
```

array_walk() is not affected by the internal array pointer of array. array_walk() will walk through the entire array regardless of pointer position.

Parameters

array

The input array

callback

Typically, callback takes on two parameters, the array parameter's value and the key/index.

Only the values of the array may potentially be changed; its structure cannot be altered, so the programmer cannot add, unset, or reorder elements. If the callback does not respect this requirement, the behavior of this function is undefined and unpredictable.

arg

If the optional arg parameter is supplied, it will be passed as the third parameter to the callback.

Return Values

Returns true

array

Creates an array

```
array(mixed ...$values): array
```

Read the section on the array type for more information on what an array is.

Parameters

values

The syntax "index => values", separated by commas, defines `index` and `values`. `index` may be of type string or integer. When `index` is omitted, an integer index is automatically generated, starting at 0. If `index` is an integer, the next generated index will be the biggest integer index + 1. Note that when two identical indexes are defined, the last overwrite the first.

Having a trailing comma after the last defined array entry, while unusual, is a valid syntax.

Return values

Returns an array of the parameters. The parameters can be given an index with the => operator. Read the section on the array type for more information on what an array is.

arsort

Sorts an array in descending order and maintains index association

```
arsort(array &$array, int $flags = SORT_REGULAR): bool
```

It sorts an array in place in descending order, such that its keys maintain their correlation with the values they are associated with. This is used mainly when sorting associative arrays where the actual element order is significant.

Parameters

array

The input array

flags

The optional second parameter flags may be used to modify the sorting behavior using these values:

Sorting type flags:

SORT_REGULAR compares items normally; the details are described in the comparison operators section.

SORT_NUMERIC compares items numerically.

SORT_STRING compares items as strings.

SORT_LOCALE_STRING compares items as strings, based on the current locale. It uses the locale, which can be changed using setlocale().

SORT_NATURAL compares items as strings using "natural ordering" like natsort().

SORT_FLAG_CASE can be combined (bitwise OR) with SORT_STRING or SORT_NATURAL to sort strings case-insensitively.

Return values

Always returns true

assort

Sorts an array in ascending order and maintains index association

```
asort(array &$array, int $flags = SORT_REGULAR): bool
```

Sorts array in place in ascending order, such that its keys maintain their correlation with the values they are associated with. This is used mainly when sorting associative arrays where the actual element order is significant.

Parameters

array

The input array

flags

The optional second parameter flags may be used to modify the sorting behavior using these values:

Sorting type flags:

SORT_REGULAR compares items normally; the details are described in the comparison operators section.

SORT_NUMERIC compares items numerically.

SORT_STRING compares items as strings.

SORT_LOCALE_STRING compares items as strings, based on the current locale. It uses the locale, which can be changed using setlocale().

SORT_NATURAL compares items as strings using "natural ordering" like natsort().

SORT_FLAG_CASE can be combined (bitwise OR) with SORT_STRING or SORT_NATURAL to sort strings case-insensitively.

Return values

Always returns true

compact

Creates array containing variables and their values

```
compact(array|string $var_name, array|string ...$var_
names): array
```

For each of these, compact() looks for a variable with that name in the current symbol table and adds it to the output array such that the variable name becomes the key and the contents of the variable become the value for that key. In short, it does the opposite of extract().

Parameters

var_name

var_names

compact() takes a variable number of parameters. Each parameter can be either a string containing the name of the variable or an array of variable names. The array can contain other arrays of variable names inside it; compact() handles it recursively.

Return values

Returns the output array with all the variables added to it

count

Counts all elements in an array or in a Countable object

```
count(Countable|array $value, int $mode = COUNT_NORMAL): int
```

When used with an object that implements the Countable interface, it returns the return value of the method Countable::count().

Parameters

    value

    An array or Countable object

    mode

If the optional mode parameter is set to COUNT_RECURSIVE (or 1), count() will recursively count the array. This is particularly useful for counting all the elements of a multidimensional array.

Caution   count() can detect recursion to avoid an infinite loop but will emit an E_WARNING every time it does (in case the array contains itself more than once) and return a count higher than may be expected.

Return values

Returns the number of elements in value. Prior to PHP 8.0.0, if the parameter was neither an array nor an object that implements the Countable interface, 1 would be returned, unless the value was null, in which case 0 would be returned.

current

Returns the current element in an array

```
current(array|object $array): mixed
```

Every array has an internal pointer to its "current" element, which is initialized to the first element inserted into the array.

Parameters

    array

    The array

Return values

The current() function simply returns the value of the array element that's currently being pointed to by the internal pointer. It does not move the pointer in any way. If the internal pointer points beyond the end of the elements list or the array is empty, current() returns false.

Warning This function may return a Boolean false but may also return a non-Boolean value that evaluates to false. Please read the section on Booleans for more information. Use the === operator for testing the return value of this function.

---

each

Returns the current key and value pair from an array and advances the array cursor

```
each(array|object &$array): array
```

After each() has executed, the array cursor will be left on the next element of the array or past the last element if it hits the end of the array. You have to use reset() if you want to traverse the array again using each.

Parameters

array

The input array

Return values

Returns the current key and value pair from the array array. This pair is returned in a four-element array, with the keys 0, 1, key, and value. Elements 0 and key contain the key name of the array element, and 1 and value contain the data.

If the internal pointer for the array points past the end of the array contents, each() returns false.

end

Sets the internal pointer of an array to its last element and returns its value.

```
end(array|object &$array): mixed
```

Parameters

array

The array. This array is passed by reference because it is modified by the function. This means you must pass it a real variable and not a function returning an array because only actual variables may be passed by reference.

Return values

Returns the value of the last element or false for empty array

extract

Imports variables into the current symbol table from an array

```
extract(array &$array, int $flags = EXTR_OVERWRITE, string
$prefix = ""): int
```

Checks each key to see whether it has a valid variable name. It also checks for collisions with existing variables in the symbol table.

Warning   Do not use `extract()` on untrusted data, like user input (e.g., `$_GET`, `$_FILES`).

Parameters

array

An associative array. This function treats keys as variable names and values as variable values. For each key/value pair, it will create a variable in the current symbol table, subject to flags and prefix parameters.

You must use an associative array; a numerically indexed array will not produce results unless you use EXTR_PREFIX_ALL or EXTR_PREFIX_INVALID.

flags

The way invalid/numeric keys and collisions are treated is determined by the extraction flags. It can be one of the following values:

EXTR_OVERWRITE

If there is a collision, overwrite the existing variable.

EXTR_SKIP

If there is a collision, don't overwrite the existing variable.

EXTR_PREFIX_SAME

If there is a collision, prefix the variable name with the prefix.

EXTR_PREFIX_ALL

Prefix all variable names with the prefix.

EXTR_PREFIX_INVALID

Only prefix invalid/numeric variable names with the prefix.

EXTR_IF_EXISTS

Only overwrite the variable if it already exists in the current symbol table; otherwise, do nothing. This is useful for defining a list of valid variables and then extracting only those variables you have defined out of $_REQUEST, for example.

EXTR_PREFIX_IF_EXISTS

Only create prefixed variable names if the non-prefixed version of the same variable exists in the current symbol table.

EXTR_REFS

Extracts variables as references. This effectively means that the values of the imported variables are still referencing the values of the array parameter. You can use this flag on its own or combine it with any other flag by OR'ing the flags.

If flags is not specified, it is assumed to be EXTR_OVERWRITE.

prefix

Note that prefix is only required if flags is EXTR_PREFIX_SAME, EXTR_ PREFIX_ALL, EXTR_PREFIX_INVALID, or EXTR_PREFIX_IF_EXISTS. If the prefixed result is not a valid variable name, it is not imported into the symbol table. Prefixes are automatically separated from the array key by an underscore character.

Return values

Returns the number of variables successfully imported into the symbol table

in_array

Checks if a value exists in an array

```
in_array(mixed $needle, array $haystack, bool $strict =
false): bool
```

Searches for needle in haystack using loose comparison unless strict is set

Parameters

needle

The searched value

Note   If needle is a string, the comparison is done in a case-sensitive manner.

---

haystack

The array

strict

If the third parameter called strict is set to true, the in_array() function will also check the types of the needle in the haystack.

Return values

Returns true if needle is found in the array and false otherwise

key_exists

Alias of array_key_exists

key

Fetches a key from an array

key(array|object $array): int|string|null

key() returns the index element of the current array position.

Parameters

array

The array

Return values

The key() function simply returns the key of the array element that is currently being pointed to by the internal pointer. It does not move the pointer in any way. If the internal pointer points beyond the end of the elements list or the array is empty, key() returns null.

krsort

Sorts an array by key in descending order

krsort(array &$array, int $flags = SORT_REGULAR): bool

Sorts an array in place by keys in descending order

Parameters

array

The input array

flags

The optional second parameter named flags may be used to modify the sorting behavior using these values:

Sorting type flags:

SORT_REGULAR compares items normally; the details are described in the comparison operators section.

SORT_NUMERIC compares items numerically.

SORT_STRING compares items as strings.

SORT_LOCALE_STRING compares items as strings, based on the current locale. It uses the locale, which can be changed using setlocale().

SORT_NATURAL compares items as strings using "natural ordering" like natsort().

SORT_FLAG_CASE can be combined (bitwise OR) with SORT_STRING or SORT_NATURAL to sort strings case-insensitively.

Return values

Always returns true

ksort

Sorts an array by key in ascending order

```
krsort(array &$array, int $flags = SORT_REGULAR): bool
```

Parameters

array

The input array

flags

The optional second parameter named flags may be used to modify the sorting behavior using these values:

Sorting type flags:

SORT_REGULAR compares items normally; the details are described in the comparison operators section.

SORT_NUMERIC compares items numerically.

SORT_STRING compares items as strings.

SORT_LOCALE_STRING compares items as strings, based on the current locale. It uses the locale, which can be changed using setlocale().

SORT_NATURAL compares items as strings using "natural ordering" like natsort().

SORT_FLAG_CASE can be combined (bitwise OR) with SORT_STRING or SORT_NATURAL to sort strings case-insensitively

Return values

Always returns true

list

Assigns variables as if they were an array

```
list(mixed $var, mixed ...$vars = ?): array
```

Like array(), this is not really a function but a language construct. list() is used to assign a list of variables in one operation. Strings can't be unpacked and list() expressions can't be completely empty.

Parameters

var

A variable

vars

Further variables

Return values

Returns the assigned array

natcasesort

Sorts an array using a case-insensitive "natural order" algorithm

```
natcasesort(array &$array): bool
```

natcasesort() is a case insensitive version of natsort(). This function implements a sort algorithm that orders alphanumeric strings in the way a human being would while maintaining key/value associations. This is described as a "natural ordering."

Parameters

array

The input array

Return values

Always returns true

natsort

Sorts an array using a "natural order" algorithm

```
natsort(array &$array): bool
```

This function implements a sort algorithm that orders alphanumeric strings in the way a human being would while maintaining key/value associations. This is described as a "natural ordering."

Parameters

array

The input array

Return values

Always returns true

next

Advances the internal pointer of an array

```
next(array|object &$array): mixed
```

next() behaves like current(), with one difference. It advances the internal array pointer one place forward before returning the element value. This means it returns the next array value and advances the internal array pointer by one.

Parameters

array

The array being affected

Return values

Returns the array value in the next place that's pointed to by the internal array pointer or false if there are no more elements.

Warning   This function may return Boolean false but may also return a non-Boolean value that evaluates to false. Please read the section on Booleans for more information. Use the === operator for testing the return value of this function.

---

pos
> Alias of current

prev

Rewinds the internal array pointer

```
prev(array|object &$array): mixed
```

prev() behaves just like next(), except it rewinds the internal array pointer one place instead of advancing it.

Parameters
> array
> The input array

Return values
> Returns the array value in the previous place that's pointed to by the internal array pointer, or false if there are no more elements.

Warning   This function may return Boolean false but may also return a non-Boolean value that evaluates to false. Please read the section on Booleans for more information. Use the === operator for testing the return value of this function.

---

range

Creates an array containing a range of elements

```
range(string|int|float $start, string|int|float $end, int|float
$step = 1): array
```

Parameters

start

First value of the sequence

end

The sequence is ended upon reaching the end value.

step

If a step value is given, it will be used as the increment (or decrement) between elements in the sequence. step must not equal 0 and must not exceed the specified range. If not specified, step will default to 1.

Return values

Returns an array of elements from start to end, inclusive

reset

Sets the internal pointer of an array to its first element

```
reset(array|object &$array): mixed
```

reset() rewinds array's internal pointer to the first element and returns the value of the first array element.

Parameters

array

The input array

Return values

Returns the value of the first array element or false if the array is empty

Warning   This function may return Boolean false but may also return a non-Boolean value that evaluates to false. Please read the section on Booleans for more information. Use the === operator for testing the return value of this function.

rsort

Sorts an array in descending order

```
rsort(array &$array, int $flags = SORT_REGULAR): bool
```

Parameters

array

The input array

flags

The optional second parameter, flags, may be used to modify the sorting behavior using these values:

Sorting type flags:

SORT_REGULAR compares items normally; the details are described in the comparison operators section.

SORT_NUMERIC compares items numerically.

SORT_STRING compares items as strings.

SORT_LOCALE_STRING compares items as strings, based on the current locale. It uses the locale, which can be changed using setlocale().

SORT_NATURAL compares items as strings using "natural ordering" like natsort().

SORT_FLAG_CASE can be combined (bitwise OR) with SORT_STRING or SORT_NATURAL to sort strings case-insensitively.

Return values

Always returns true

shuffle

Shuffles an array

```
shuffle(array &$array): bool
```

This function shuffles (randomizes the order of the elements in) an array. It uses a pseudo random number generator that is not suitable for cryptographic purposes.

Parameters

array

The array

Return values

Returns true on success or false on failure.

sizeof

Alias of count

sort

Sorts an array in place in ascending order

```
sort(array &$array, int $flags = SORT_REGULAR): bool
```

Parameters

array

The input array

flags

The optional second parameter, flags, may be used to modify the sorting behavior using these values:

Sorting type flags:

SORT_REGULAR compares items normally; the details are described in the comparison operators section.

SORT_NUMERIC compares items numerically.

SORT_STRING compares items as strings.

SORT_LOCALE_STRING compares items as strings, based on the current locale. It uses the locale, which can be changed using setlocale().

SORT_NATURAL compares items as strings using "natural ordering" like natsort().

SORT_FLAG_CASE can be combined (bitwise OR) with SORT_STRING or SORT_NATURAL to sort strings case-insensitively.

Return values

Always returns true

uasort

Sorts an array with a user-defined comparison function and maintains index association

```
uasort(array &$array, callable $callback): bool
```

Sorts array in place such that its keys maintain their correlation with the values they are associated with, using a user-defined comparison function. This is used mainly when sorting associative arrays where the actual element order is significant.

Parameters

array

The input array

callback

The comparison function must return an integer less than, equal to, or greater than zero if the first argument is considered to be respectively less than, equal to, or greater than the second.

```
callback(mixed $a, mixed $b): int
```

Return values

Always returns true

uksort

Sorts an array by keys using a user-defined comparison function

```
uksort(array &$array, callable $callback): bool
```

Parameters

array

The input array

callback

The comparison function must return an integer less than, equal to, or greater than zero if the first argument is considered to be respectively less than, equal to, or greater than the second.

```
callback(mixed $a, mixed $b): int
```

Return values

Always returns true

usort

Sorts an array by values using a user-defined comparison function

```
usort(array &$array, callable $callback): bool
```

Parameters

array

The input array

callback

The comparison function must return an integer less than, equal to, or greater than zero if the first argument is considered to be respectively less than, equal to, or greater than the second.

```
callback(mixed $a, mixed $b): int
```

Return values

Always returns true

Summary

Overall, arrays can be as simplistic or as complex as you desire. Once you get comfortable with them, they are a great tool to have in your toolbox.

In this chapter, you learned how to hold multiple values of similar types in a single variable using PHP arrays, which can be indexed, associative, and multidimensional. You also learned about the most common PHP array functions.

In the next chapter, you will learn how to use sessions, which are used in PHP to keep track of your activity in applications, and cookies, which are used to store limited data like a user's identity.

CHAPTER 7

Sessions and Cookies

In the previous chapters, you learned how to use arrays, one of the most versatile and useful elements in PHP, to store multiple values within a single variable. Let's now imagine you need to store some information to be used across multiple web pages. You need to store some information on a local computer (client side) or store some information on a server (server side) for just a certain time using the web page. How would you do this? By using sessions and cookies.

The main difference between sessions and cookies is that cookies, as previously said, are used to store some user information on a local computer as client-side files while sessions are server-side files that store user information on a web server.

While cookies expire right after the specified lifetime you define, sessions end when you close the web browser or when you log out of the web page or program.

This chapter consists of the following sections:

- PHP Sessions
- PHP Cookies

PHP Sessions

Sessions are what PHP uses to keep track of your activity on applications. For example, when you log into an application, make some changes, upload some images, and then leave the site, that's a session.

© Gunnard Engebreth, Satej Kumar Sahu 2023
G. Engebreth and S. K. Sahu, *PHP 8 Basics*, https://doi.org/10.1007/978-1-4842-8082-9_7

The application knows who you are and has been passing around and keeping track of a variable ($_SESSION) the whole time. Session variables hold information about individual users and are passed around the application to keep track of user activity.

Unlike normal variables, sessions need to be initiated in order to maintain integrity. To do this, PHP has a session_start() function. After this, session variables are set with the $_SESSION global variable.

Let's make a simple page with a basic session declaration. Open the chapter7 folder and the first_session.php file.

```php
<?php
// Start the session
session_start();
?>
<!DOCTYPE html>
<html>
<body>

<?php
// Set session variables
$_SESSION["firstname"] = "Foo";
$_SESSION["username"] = "barFoo";
echo "Session variables are set.";
?>

</body>
</html>
```

So, session data has been set, but where is it? Sessions are stored on the server side so you can't view them through methods such as inspect element. You can, however, use var_dump() to ensure that they are stored correctly.

Go browse back to chapter7 and open first_session2.php.

Great! So now you are saving session variables. For the real test, go back to chapter7 and find session_test.php. If you can open up a brand new page and still recall the session data, then you have success. All you need to do in session_test.php is use the start_session() function to access the session data. Go ahead and click session_test.php to view the data.

```php
<?php
session_start();
?>
<!DOCTYPE html>
<html>
<body>

<?php
// Echo session variables that were set on previous page
echo "Favorite color is " . $_SESSION["favcolor"] . ".<br>";
echo "Favorite animal is " . $_SESSION["favanimal"] . ".";
?>

</body>
</html>
```

And for your last trick, let's view the session variables and then destroy them! This will remove the session information that is currently active from the use of session_start().

Click remove_session.php in the chapter7 directory to view and remove the session data. Here is what remove_session.php looks like:

```php
<?php
session_start();
?>
<!DOCTYPE html>
<html>
<body>
```

```php
<?php
echo "Here are the variables:<br />";
var_dump($_SESSION);
echo "<br /><br />";
// remove all session variables
session_unset();
echo "Here are the variables after session_unset:<br />";
var_dump($_SESSION);
echo "<br /><br />";

// destroy the session
session_destroy();
echo "Here are the variables after session_destroy:<br />";
var_dump($_SESSION);
echo "<br /><br />";
?>

</body>
</html>
```

Let's take this concept and put it into a real-life situation, like a login page connected to a database. http://localhost/chapter7/ will show you a file called seedDB.php. Go ahead and click it. You will use this file to seed your database with some information. If all is working properly, you should see output in your browser that shows

```
Seeing Users into table..1..2..3
Users added
1 - tom - hanks - 1234 - 2022-04-15 17:39:21
2 - billy - mitchell - 1234 - 2022-04-15 17:39:21
3 - mega - man - 1234 - 2022-04-15 17:39:21
```

This is the test data you can use for this example. Open up login.php and take a look at the code.

```php
<?php
// to Start a PHP session
session_start();
?>
<html>
<body>
    <div class="container">
            <form method="post" action="">
                <div id="div_login">
                        <h1>Login</h1>
                        <div>
                            <input type="text"
                            class="textbox" id="first_
                            name" name="first_name"
                            placeholder="first_name" />
                        </div>
                        <div>
                            <input type="password"
                            class="textbox"
                            id="password"
                            name="password"
                            placeholder="Password"/>
                        </div>
                        <div>
                            <input type="submit"
                            value="Submit" name="submit"
                            id="submit" />
                        </div>
                </div>
            </form>
    </div>

<?php
```

```php
// DB Host name
$host = "mysql-db";

// DB User
$user = "user";

// DB Password
$password = "pass";

// Database name
$db = "beginningPHP";

$connection = mysqli_connect($host, $user, $password, $db);

// If the connection fails
if (!$connection) {

    // Display message and terminate script
    die("Connection failed: " . mysqli_connect_error());
}

// If the submit button is pressed
if(isset($_POST['submit'])){

    // Escape special characters in a string
        $first_name = mysqli_real_escape_string($connection,
        $_POST['first_name']);
        $password = mysqli_real_escape_string($connection,
        $_POST['password']);

    // If username and password are not empty
        if ($first_name != "" && $password != ""){

        // Query database to find user with matching username
        and password
```

```php
    $query = "select count(*) as countUser from
    users where first_name='".$first_name."' and
    password='".$password."'";

// Store query result
    $result = mysqli_query($connection, $query);

// Fetch row as associative array
    $row = mysqli_fetch_array($result);

// Get number of rows
    $count = $row['countUser'];

// If number of row is more than zero
    if($count > 0){

    // Set matched user as current user
            $_SESSION['first_name'] = $first_name;
            $_SESSION['timestamp'] = date("h:i:sa");

    // Display success message
        echo "You are logged in!";
            if (isset($_SESSION)) {
                echo "<br /><br />";
                print_r($_SESSION);
            }

// Else if number of row is less than zero
    } else {

    // Display failed message
            echo "Error! Invalid first_name and
            password.";
    }

}
```

```
}
?>
</body>
</html>
```

Let's break this down line by line.

```
<?php
// to Start a PHP session
session_start();
```

Here you are using the session_start() function to start your session.

```
?>
<html>
<body>
    <div class="container">
            <form method="post" action="">
                <div id="div_login">
                        <h1>Login</h1>
                        <div>
                            <input type="text"
                            class="textbox" id="first_
                            name" name="first_name"
                            placeholder="first_name" />
                        </div>
                        <div>
                            <input type="password"
                            class="textbox"
                            id="password"
                            name="password"
                            placeholder="Password"/>
                        </div>
```

```
            <div>
                <input type="submit"
                value="Submit" name="submit"
                id="submit" />
            </div>
        </div>
    </form>
```

This is your basic form that you will use to gather the credentials from your user. Use consistent naming with the database for easier tracking. This can be anything from "username"/"password" to "user"/"secret."

```
    </div>
```

```php
<?php
// DB Host name
$host = "mysql-db";

// DB User
$user = "user";

// DB Password
$password = "pass";

// Database name
$db = "beginningPHP";

$connection = mysqli_connect($host, $user, $password, $db);
```

This connects to your database using the credentials that will be used throughout this book. Below, you check for the connection and show an error if it fails for any reason:

```php
// If the connection fails
if (!$connection) {
```

```
    // Display message and terminate script
    die("Connection failed: " . mysqli_connect_error());
}

// If the submit button is pressed
if(isset($_POST['submit'])){

    // Escape special characters in a string
        $first_name = mysqli_real_escape_string($connection,
        $_POST['first_name']);
        $password = mysqli_real_escape_string($connection,
        $_POST['password']);

    // If username and password are not empty
        if ($first_name != "" && $password != ""){
```

You need to check the input and sanitize it before introducing it to the database. This will help prevent MySQL injection attacks.

```
            $query = "select count(*) as countUser from
            users where first_name='".$first_name."' and
            password='".$password."'";
```

Here is your query to check if the first_name value in the database is equal to $first_name from the form.

```
    // Store query result
        $result = mysqli_query($connection, $query);

    // Fetch row as associative array
        $row = mysqli_fetch_array($result);

    // Get number of rows
        $count = $row['countUser'];

    // If number of row is more than zero
```

```php
if($count > 0){

    // Set matched user as current user
            $_SESSION['first_name'] = $first_name;
            $_SESSION['timestamp'] = date("h:i:sa");

    // Display success message
        echo "You are logged in!";
            if (isset($_SESSION)) {
                echo "<br /><br />";
                print_r($_SESSION);
            }

    // Else if number of row is less than zero
        } else {

    // Display failed message
            echo "Error! Invalid first_name and
            password.";
        }

    }

}
?>
</body>
</html>
```

Use the test data "tom" and password "1234" to test. You can always go back to the chapter7 directory and run remove_session.php to clear out or log out the session data.

Please note that for preventing SQL injection you can use PDO (PHP data objects), which is an abstraction layer that can be used for database queries as an alternative to MySQLi.

PHP Cookies

Cookies are often used to identify a user. A cookie is a small file that is embedded on the user's computer by the server. Remember that session variables are stored on the server, unlike cookies. Each time the same computer requests a page, the cookie is available for the application to read and identify the user. PHP can be used to both create and retrieve these cookie values.

Similar to sessions, you need to make use of a built-in PHP function named setcookie() to begin using them. The syntax for setting a cookie is

setcookie(name, value, expire, path, domain, secure, httponly);

Name is the only required value. Go a head and open first_cookie.php from chapter7 and look at the code.

```php
<?php
$cookie_name = "username";
$cookie_value = "Betchy McCleaver";
setcookie($cookie_name, $cookie_value, time() + (86400 * 30),
"/"); // 86400 = 1 day
?>
<html>
<body>

<?php
if(!isset($_COOKIE[$cookie_name])) {
  echo "Cookie named '" . $cookie_name . "' is not set!";
} else {
  echo "Cookie '" . $cookie_name . "' is set!<br>";
  echo "Value is: " . $_COOKIE[$cookie_name];
}
?>
```

In this example, you are creating a cookie named username and setting the value to Betchy McCleaver (my eighth-grade science teacher). The expiration date of the cookie is 30 days. You come to this value by multiplying 86,400 (the total number of seconds in 24 hours/one day) by 30 (the length in days that you want the cookie to stay valid). Next, you set which part of your website can access the cookie: / , meaning any PHP application from the domain. To retrieve the cookie, much like $_SESSION, you use $_COOKIE.

Go to the chapter7 directory on your localhost in the browser and click first_cookie.php. You will see that it says the cookie is not set. This is because it is the first time you've run the script. Press refresh and you will see the cookie! You can verify the cookie through inspect element in your browser. Right-click the page and press inspect element and then click Application on the top right side and then Cookies on the left column, as shown in Figure 7-1.

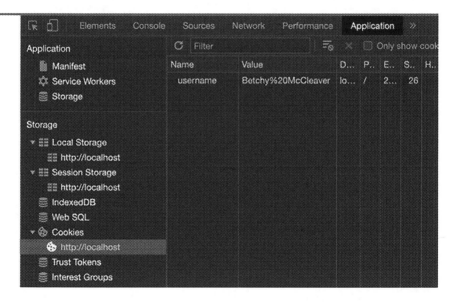

Figure 7-1. *Inspection element page to check on cookie information*

Now let's modify a cookie.

Open up `modify_cookie.php.` Change the value of `username` to `Jason Bourne`. You can verify this by refreshing the page or by the `inspect element` method above.

To delete a cookie, you basically invalidate the time. The cookie is created but set to a past date for expiration. This will invalidate and remove the cookie from your system.

```php
<?php
// set the expiration date to one hour ago
setcookie("username", "", time() - 3600);
?>
<html>
<body>

<?php
echo "Cookie 'user' is deleted.";
?>

</body>
</html>
```

You can click `delete_cookie.php` for a working example of this.

A good habit to get into is to check if cookies are enabled before relying on them.

```php
<?php
setcookie("test_cookie", "test", time() + 3600, '/');
?>
<html>
<body>

<?php
if(count($_COOKIE) > 0) {
  echo "Cookies are enabled.";
```

```
} else {
  echo "Cookies are disabled.";
}
?>

</body>
</html>
```

Here you attempt to set an arbitrary cookie and then read it. If you can verify that the cookie is set, you know the user has cookies enabled!

Summary

In this chapter, you learned how to use sessions and cookies in the PHP language to keep track of your activity on web applications. You saw how to create, store, and manage information in PHP sessions and cookies.

In the next chapter, you will learn how to use PHP objects, which are another compound data type. They are similar to arrays, which can be set and used with multiple types of information, from strings to all types of numbers.

CHAPTER 8

Objects

So far, we have covered several data types, including the string, integer, and float. You've learned how to use strings, integers, and arrays. Each of these types has their own benefits and limitations. An integer cannot use the letter "s" as a value, and a string can contain an integer of "1." With arrays, you learned about the idea of a compound data type. This data type allows for combining and intermixing of different elements. An array can contain both letters and numbers, contain specific key-pair values (associative array), or just contain an organized set of data. The end result is that values of more than one type can be stored together in a single variable.

In this brief chapter, we will focus on a PHP data type we touched on in Chapters 2 and 4: the object.

Please notice that, in general, classes and objects are the two main aspects of object-oriented programming and are therefore very important.

To understand how classes and objects are interlinked, we could say that a class is a template for an object and an object is an instance of a certain class.

Similar to arrays, you can set and use multiple types of information, from strings to all types of numbers. Objects, however, give you the ability to define specific functionality. This functionality is set in the class definition.

So, when you create an individual object, it will inherit all the properties and behaviors from the class it's linked to, but each object will still have different values for the properties.

Objects are user-defined classes that can store both values and functions and must be explicitly declared.

Let's take a look at some basic examples.

© Gunnard Engebreth, Satej Kumar Sahu 2023
G. Engebreth and S. K. Sahu, *PHP 8 Basics*, https://doi.org/10.1007/978-1-4842-8082-9_8

```php
<?php
class Vegetable {
  // Properties
  public $name;
  public $color;

  // Methods
  function set_name($name) {
    $this->name = $name;
  }
  function get_name() {
    return $this->name;
  }
}
?>
```

Here you are declaring a class named Vegetable. This class contains both properties and methods. Remember that properties are variables and methods are functions. The two properties are $name and $color. The two methods are set_name and get_name. They are commonly referred to as "getters and setters." These types of methods are common with objects because you are constantly "getting" and "setting" values to the class properties. It is very convenient to create these helper type functions. If you have these functions in your objects, you will only need to remember to $vegetable->get_name(); and $vegetable->set_name();.

Here is another example of an object:

```php
<?php
class SayHi{
    function hi(){
        echo "Hello World";
    }
}
```

```
$obj=new SayHi;
$obj->hi();
?>
```

Output: Hello World

In some cases, you may want to create an object on the fly. PHP has stdClass, which allows you to do this.

```
<?php
$obj=new stdClass;
$obj->name="gunnard";
$obj->age=26;
$obj->twitter="@gunnard";
print_r($obj);
?>
```

Output

This will produce following result:

```
stdClass Object(
    [name] => gunnard
    [age] => 26
    [twitter] => @gunnard
)
```

Let's start fresh with a basic class and see how changes in the class affect the object. You will create a Beverage class to classify and track information on beverages at the pizzeria that you run.

```php
<?php
class Beverage {
    public $name;
    public $type;
    public $temperature;
    public $price;
    public $sale;
}
```

In order to use this class as an object, you need to instantiate it. This is done through the new keyword.

```php
<?php
$cola = new Beverage();
?>
```

Now you have an object with the name $cola, which contains the properties you defined in the class Beverage. You can use this object by assigning values to the properties with the -> operator. This will allow you to assign specific values to each property.

```php
<?php
$cola = new Beverage();
$cola->name = "Rocky Cola";
$cola->type = "Soda";
$cola->teperature = "45 f";
$cola->price = "0.50";
$cola->sale = null;
?>
```

Now that you can set values to your class properties, let's add class methods or functions within a class that allow objects to manipulate data. For example,

```php
<?php
class Beverage {
    public $name;
    public $type;
    public $temperature;
    public $price;
    public $sale;
}

function getMenuName() {
    return $this->type:.' '.$this->name.' '.$this->price;
}

?>
```

With getMenuName, the intention is to display the type, name, and price of the beverage. This can be used when displaying the full menu of the restaurant. Instead of using the object to return the name, type, and price, and THEN formatting it, you can take care of all of that in this method.

The $this variable refers to the current object in use. When you invoke the getMenuName() method, $this refers to the specific object that calls the method. Object methods are accessed similarly to properties, using the object operator ->, but as with any function, there are parentheses at the end, as in ().

Summary

In this chapter, you learned how to use a PHP object, which is another compound data type. It is similar to an array, which can be set and use with multiple types of information, from strings to all types of numbers.

In the next chapter, you will learn how ...

CHAPTER 9

PHP Exceptions, Validation, and Regular Expressions

PHP is indeed one of the most used programming languages in the world to develop applications and websites on the Internet. PHP 8 is a very dynamic, flexible programming language; it's also easy to use as embedded language, for instance, for HTML.

In this chapter, you will learn all about exceptions, form validation, and regular expressions. What are they and when do we need to use them?

PHP is indeed very flexibility programming language, also when it comes to handling exceptions, which are out-of-the-ordinary scenarios that may occur in code. A code exception can be something like an input or code bug, and PHP version 8, compared to previous versions, has been updated to be more secure and to handle more exceptions better.

We will explain how to use PHP exceptions using `try`, `catch`, and `throw`.

Also, as developer, you will need to do web form validation, which means validating certain values entered in a PHP form of various input field types like text boxes, checkboxes, radio buttons, and checklists.

© Gunnard Engebreth, Satej Kumar Sahu 2023
G. Engebreth and S. K. Sahu, *PHP 8 Basics*, https://doi.org/10.1007/978-1-4842-8082-9_9

Finally, we will describe the usage of PHP regular expressions, which are simply a sequence of characters that form a search pattern and can be used, for instance, to check with your PHP code if a provided string of text contains a certain pattern of characters.

This chapter consists of the following sections:

- PHP Exceptions (try, catch, finally, and throw)

- PHP Form Validation (validating Name and E-Mail values)

- PHP Regular Expressions

PHP Exceptions

As we said in the introduction of the chapter, an exception in a programming language is simply an unexpected outcome of a PHP program. Your goal is to tell your code how to handle any unexpected outcome by itself, where possible.

Please remember that the main difference between an error and an exception is that an exception will disrupt the normal flow of your code but by adding some additional code it can be handled while an error cannot be handled by the code itself. You will see how to use PHP to handle exceptions thrown and catch them.

PHP, like all programming languages, must have a code exception mechanism to handle runtime errors, also known exceptions. This, in PHP and any other language, is necessary to maintain the normal flow of the application.

Each language includes a set of throwable exceptions and errors. In PHP, there are many different types of errors that may occur in your code. Here are some:

- CompileError

- ParseError

- TypeError

- ArithmeticError

PHP also include an exception called implements throwable, which can be the following:

- ClosedGeneratorException: Occurs when trying to attempt to perform a traversal on a generator that has already been closed or terminated.

- DOMException: When an operation is impossible to perform for logical reasons

- ErrorException: Used to convert a PHP error to an exception

- IntlException: As per the PHP documentation, this class is used for generating exceptions when errors occur inside an intl function. Such exceptions are only generated when intl.use_exceptions is enabled.

PHP can help us handle runtime errors such as IOException, SQLException, ClassNotFoundException, and many more.

Let's start with an example where unfortunately the exception is not caught, generating a fatal error issued with an "Uncaught Exception" message.

In this example, you will throw an exception without catching it by sending the number 3 to a PHP function named checkMyNum, which is expecting only a value of 1 or below.

Here is the code:

Chapter9/exception1.php

```php
<?php
//here we create a function with an exception
function checkMyNum($mynumber) {
  if($mynumber>1) {
    throw new Exception("The entered number must be 1 or
    below!!");
  }
  return true;
}

checkMyNum(3);
?>
```

**Fatal error: Uncaught exception 'Exception'
with message The entered number must be 1 or below!!' in C:\
mytest.php:5
Stack trace: #0 C:\mytest.php(11):
checkMyNum(3) #1 {main} thrown in C:\mytest.php on line 5**

To fix this error, let's see how to handle and correct the above uncaught exception error by using PHP exception handling ways named try, catch, and throw.

- try: The try block includes your function triggered in the case of an exception of your code. If no exception triggers the try, the code will simply continue as normal. If an exception is triggered, it means that the exception is "thrown."

- throw: This is how you trigger a certain exception but remember that each throw must have at least one catch in the code.

- catch: The catch block mainly retrieves the exception occurred and creates an object containing the exception information and decides what to do, like print an error message.

- finally: The finally block can be specified after or instead of a catch block. The code within the finally block will always be executed after the try and catch blocks, regardless of whether an exception has been thrown and before normal execution resumes.

The syntax of the try...catch...finally block looks like this:

```php
<?php
try {
    // do something in our code
} catch (Exception $e) {
    // code to handle any exception
} finally {
    // code to clean up the resource and complete the code
execution
}
```

In general, this is what happens when you run the code and an exception is triggered:

- The current state of your code will be saved.

- The execution of your code will be switched automatically to the predefined exception handler function you added in the code.

- Finally, the handler function will halt the execution of program, will either resume the execution from the last saved code state, or continue the execution of your code from another part of it.

Let's now take your uncaught exception error PHP code and fix it with try, catch, finally, and throw methods.

Chapter9/exception2.php

```php
<?php
//here we create a function with an exception
function checkMyNum($mynumber) {
  if($mynumber>1) {
    throw new Exception("The entered number must be 1 or
    below!!");
  }
  return true;
}

//let's trigger the exception in a "try" block sending the
number 3
try {
  checkMyNum(3);
  //In the case of the exception thrown, this text will not be
  shown to the user
  echo 'The number you entered is 1 or below!!';
}

//our code will catch exception and generate a message
catch(Exception $e) {
echo 'Caught exception: ',  $e->getMessage(), "\n";

}

// finally block to complete our code execution process
finally {
    echo "Code execution completed.";
}

?>
```

The output of this code is the following:

**Caught exception: The entered number must be 1 or below!!
Code execution completed.**

Let's explain the code.

- You create a checkMyNum() function, which simply checks if a number is greater than 1.

- Since you sent the number 3, the exception within the checkMyNum() function is thrown

- The checkMyNum() function is called in the try block.

- Your code in the catch block will simply retrieve the exception and create the object ($e) that contains the exception information, in your case to print the "Caught exception" error message using echo, which finally will print the error message from the exception by calling $e->getMessage().

- The finally block will complete your code, just closing the code execution and writing the message "Code execution completed."

Please remember that you can develop your own PHP customized exception handler by just creating a special class with functions that can be called when a certain exception occurs in your PHP code. This customized exception handler class must be an extension of the exception class.

Let's see next how to validate a PHP web form.

PHP Form Validation

Web form validation at the client side is very important for security reasons, helping developers protect PHP forms from hackers and spammers.

You may need to perform a PHP form validation of the values entered in a PHP form containing various types of fields like text boxes, checkboxes, radio buttons, and checklists.

Say you have an HTML web form and you want to use PHP to validate the values entered in the form prior sending it to the server.

First, build a simple HTML web form like this:

Chapter9/form-action.html

```
<!DOCTYPE HTML>
<html>
<head>
</head>
<body>
<h2>PHP Form Validation</h2>
<form  method="post" action="form-action.php" >
  Name: <input type="text" name="name">
  <br><br>
  E-mail: <input type="text" name="email">
  <br><br>
    <input type="submit" name="submit" value="Submit">
</form>
</body>
</html>
```

When you run your HTML form, it will look like Figure 9-1.

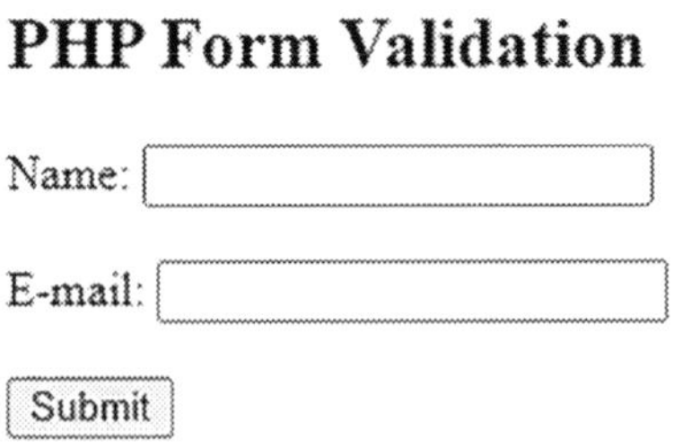

PHP Form Validation

Name: [   ]

E-mail: [   ]

[Submit]

Figure 9-1. *HTML form web page*

Now you need to write some PHP code that will allow you to simply verify the values entered as Name and E-mail before they are sent to the server.

Suppose you wish to have the HTML value of Name required and that it must only contain letters and whitespace. The E-mail value will also be required and must contain a valid email address (including @ and . as typical email format characters).

Let's start from the previous HTML web page and add some PHP validation code. Create a new PHP file named form-action.php, which for now will only validate if the values entered are not empty:

Chapter9/form-action.php

```
<!DOCTYPE HTML>
<html>
<head>
<style>
.error {color: #FF0000;}
</style>
</head>
<body>

<?php
$name = "";
$email = "";

$nameError = "";
$emailError = "";

  if (empty($_POST["name"])) {
    $nameError = "Name is required";
  }

  if (empty($_POST["email"])) {
    $emailError = "Email is required";
  }

?>
```

```
<h2>PHP Form Validation</h2>
<p><span class="error">* required field</span></p>
<form  method="post" action="form-action.php" >
  Name: <input type="text" name="name">
  <span class="error">* <?php echo $nameError;?></span>
  <br><br>
  E-mail: <input type="text" name="email">
  <span class="error">* <?php echo $emailError;?></span>
  <br><br>
  <input type="submit" name="submit" value="Submit">
</form>

</body>
</html>
```

When you run your PHP file, it will look like Figure 9-2.

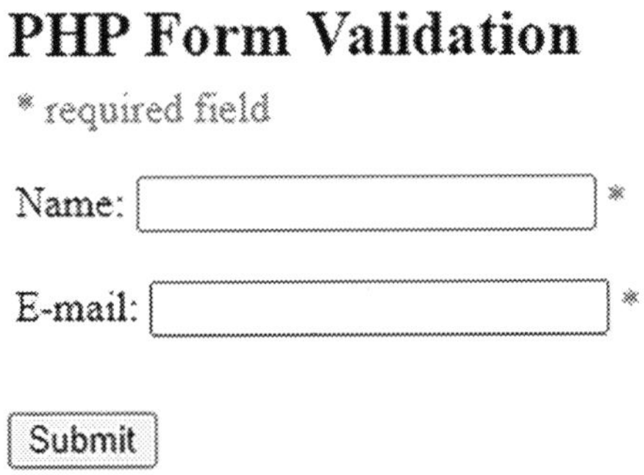

Figure 9-2. *PHP form web page*

As you can see, the web form informs you that the Name and E-mail fields are required and therefore cannot be empty. When you try to submit the form with one or both fields empty, you will get the error messages shown in Figure 9-3.

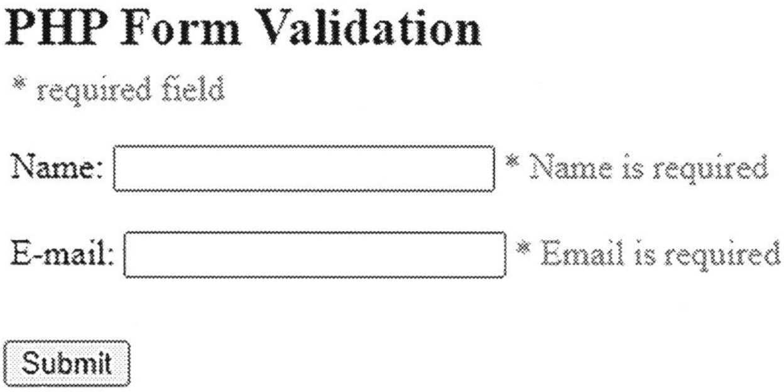

PHP Form Validation

* required field

Name: [_____] * Name is required

E-mail: [_____] * Email is required

[Submit]

Figure 9-3. *PHP form web page submitted with empty fields*

Let's update the PHP example so that it will validate the value entered for Name, which must only be letters and whitespace, and validate that the format of the E-mail value must contain @ and . characters as part of the value submitted.

Here is the updated code:

Chapter9/form-action.php

```php
<!DOCTYPE HTML>
<html>
<head>
<style>
.error {color: #FF0000;}
</style>
</head>
<body>

<?php
$name = "";
$nameError = "";

$email = "";
$emailError = "";

  if (empty($_POST["name"])) {
    $nameError = "Name is required";
```

```php
  } else {
    $name = test_input($_POST["name"]);
    if (!preg_match("/^[a-zA-Z-' ]*$/",$name)) {
      $nameError = "Error: Only letters and whitespace
      allowed!";
    }
  }

  if (empty($_POST["email"])) {
    $emailError = "Email is required";
  } else {
    $email = test_input($_POST["email"]);
    if (!filter_var($email, FILTER_VALIDATE_EMAIL)) {
      $emailError = "Error: Invalid email format!";
    }
  }

?>


<h2>PHP Form Validation</h2>
<p><span class="error">* required field</span></p>
<form  method="post" action="form-action.php" >
  Name: <input type="text" name="name">
  <span class="error">* <?php echo $nameError;?></span>
  <br><br>
  E-mail: <input type="text" name="email">
  <span class="error">* <?php echo $emailError;?></span>
  <br><br>
  <input type="submit" name="submit" value="Submit">
</form>

</body>
</html>
```

Rerun your PHP file. Now, just entering some special characters in the Name field and entering the E-mail value with no @ or . characters will result in error messages that the characters are not allowed and the email format is invalid. See Figure 9-4.

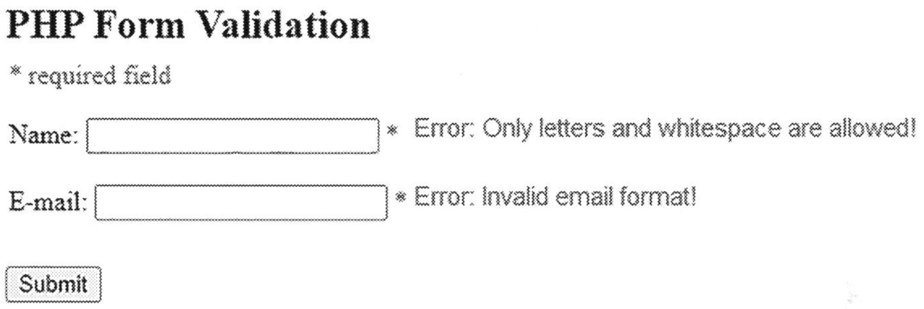

PHP Form Validation

* required field

Name: [_____] * Error: Only letters and whitespace are allowed!

E-mail: [_____] * Error: Invalid email format!

[Submit]

Figure 9-4. *PHP form web page submitted with invalid values*

When you analyze the code, you see that to validate the Name value, you utilize the PHP regular expression function `preg_match()` (you will learn more about it later in this chapter), which returns 1 if the pattern is found in the string and 0 if it is not.

So, in your PHP code you define the function as `preg_match("/^[a-zA-Z-' ]*$/",$name)`, where you force the value entered to have only letters and whitespace. If not, the code will produce an error message of "Error: Only letters and whitespace allowed!"

To validate the E-mail value, you use the PHP function named `filter_var()`, which filters a variable with a specified filter and utilizes the PHP predefined filter constant `FILTER_VALIDATE_EMAIL`, which validates a value as a valid format for an entered e-mail address.

If you didn't enter @ or ., the code will produce the error "Error: Invalid email format!"

Let's now learn how to use PHP regular expressions.

PHP Regular Expressions

As we said in the introduction of the chapter, a regular expression is simply a sequence of characters that forms a searching pattern. Regular expressions are commonly known as **regex** and by default they are case-sensitive.

In general, a regular expression can be a single character or a more complicated pattern made of several characters.

They are mainly used when you need to run a text search, perform a text replace operation, or split a string into multiple chunks, for instance.

Regular expressions use arithmetic operators (+, -, ^) to create complex expressions.

Consider using regular expressions when

- You need to validate a certain text string in your code.

- You need to analyze and search a pattern in a certain string or modify a text string.

- You need to search for special keywords.

- You need help with user input validation testing, validating browser detection, spamming filtration, password strength checking, and more.

The PHP regular expression syntax looks like this:

```
$pattern = "/mas[si]mo/i";
$text = "My name is Massimo.";
```

where

- / is the delimiter .

- mas[si]mo is the pattern you are searching for.

- i is an example of a special character you can use with a regular expression (in this case, it forces case-insensitive searching).

- [si]: This square bracket defines which character within a certain pattern might or might not be searched (in this case, it means match one character, s or i).

- @Text is the given string you will search the pattern in.

In regular expressions, the delimiter can be any character, but it cannot be a letter, number, backslash, or space.

Regular Expressions Modifiers

Regular expressions utilize special characters named modifiers to define how the search is performed. They include

- i: When you need to have a case-insensitive pattern search

- m: When you need to perform a multiline search using a pattern to search at the beginning or end of a string to match

- u: When you need to enable a correct matching of UTF-8 encoded patterns

Regular Expression Metacharacters

Regular expression syntax includes the use of special characters, also called metacharacters, with certain special meanings:

- \ is a general escape character with several uses.

- ^ means to assert start of subject (or line, in multiline mode).

- $ means to assert end of subject or before a terminating newline (or end of line, in multiline mode).

- . means match any character except newline (by default).

- [means start character class definition.

-] means end character class definition.

- | means the start of an alternative branch.

- (means start a subpattern.

-) means end a subpattern.

- ? extends the meaning of (, also 0 or 1 quantifier, also makes greedy quantifiers lazy (see repetition).

- * is used for 0 or more quantifiers.

- + is used for 1 or more quantifiers.

- { is a start min/max quantifier.

- } is an end min/max quantifier.

Regular Expression Square Brackets

In a regular expression, square brackets surrounding a pattern of characters are called a character class, So [abcdef] will match a single character out of your list of specified characters. In this example of a regular expression, [abcdef] will only match the a, b, c, d , e, or f characters and nothing else.

Here is how square brackets can be used with regular expressions:

- [abc] means match one character from the options in the brackets.

- [^abc] means match any character NOT in the brackets.

- [0-9] means match one character from the range 0 to 9.

Regular Expression Quantifiers

Regular expressions also include so-called quantifiers to specify the specific number of times that a character or a group of characters can be repeated in a regular expression. Here are some examples:

- a+ matches any string that contains at least one character a.

- a* matches any string that contains zero or more occurrences of the character a.

- a{x} matches any string that contains the letter a exactly x times.

- a{2} matches any string that contains the letter a exactly two times.

- a{x,y} matches any string that contains a between x and y times.

Finally, PHP regular expressions use grouping via parentheses to apply quantifiers to entire patterns.

Regular Expression Functions

Let's have a look now at the major regular expression functions that are used with PHP:

- preg_match() returns 1 if the pattern is found in the string and 0 if it is not.

- preg_match_all() returns the number of how many times the pattern was found in the string or false on failure.

- preg_replace() returns a new string where matched patterns have been replaced with another string; otherwise, the subject is returned unchanged or null if an error occurrs.

Let's start your first example of PHP regular expression using preg_match(), which will return 1 if the pattern is found in the string and 0 if it is not. Here is the code:

Chapter 9 (regexpress1.php)

```php
<?php
$pattern = "/massimo/i";
$text = "My name is Massimo.";
if(preg_match($pattern, $text)){
    echo "Match was found!"; }
else{
    echo "Match was not found."; }
?>
```

The output of this code is **Match was found!** because "Massimo" is in the text and the i means case-insensitive, which means "Massimo" and "Massimo" are the same.

Removing the i from the pattern means a match will be not found because regular expressions are by default case-sensitive.

Let's have the same example but using some squared brackets.

Chapter 9/regexpress2.php

```php
<?php
$pattern = "/mas[trgs]imo/i";
$text = "My name is Massimo.";
if(preg_match($pattern, $text)){
    echo "Match was found!"; }
else{
    echo "Match was not found."; }
?>
```

The output of this code is **Match was found!** as "Massimo" is in the text, with the i meaning case-insensitive but in this case one of the needed characters, s, is in the square bracket of [trgs], which means match one character from the options in the brackets. Since s is in the square bracket, the pattern is found.

Here's an example using the metacharacter $, which means look for a match at the end of the string:

Chapter9/regexpress3.php

```php
<?php
$pattern = "/imo$/";
$text = "Massimo";
if(preg_match($pattern, $text)){
    echo "Match was found!"; }
else{
    echo "Match was not found."; }
?>
```

The output of this code is **Match was found!** as the pattern "imo" is found at the end of the text "Massimo."

Let's create an example of a regular expression with a group and quantifier. You want to search for a match in a string that contains the letters "co" exactly two times.

Chapter9/regexpress4.php

```php
<?php
$pattern = "/(co){2}/i";
$text = "I like coconut.";
if(preg_match($pattern, $text)){
    echo "Match was found!"; }
else{
    echo "Match was not found."; }
?>
```

The output of this code is **Match was found!** because the pattern "co" is found exactly two times in the text "I love coconut."

Let's create a new PHP example of a regular expression using `preg_match_all()`, which will return the number of how many times the pattern was found in the string.

Chapter9/regexpress5.php

```php
<?php
$pattern = "/na/i";
$text = "My name is Massimo and I was born in Naples";
echo preg_match_all($pattern, $text);
?>
```

The output of this code is **2** because the pattern "na" is found two times: in the words "name" and "Naples," because you added I so the case is insensitive.

Finally, let's create a new PHP example of a regular expression using `preg_replace()`, which returns a very new string where matched patterns are replaced with another string.

Chapter9/regexpress6.php

```php
<?php
$pattern = "/red/i";
$text = "My favorite color is red!";
echo preg_replace($pattern, "blue", $text);
?>
```

The output of this code is **"My favorite color is blue!"** because the pattern "red" is found in the text and is replaced with the new text "blue." The case is insensitive because you added i.

Summary

In this chapter, you first learned about PHP proper exceptions and how to deal with them using the `try,` `throw`, and `catch` methods. Then you saw how to use PHP to validate client HTML form values entered before sending the value to the server. Finally, you learned about PHP regular expressions, which are used almost everywhere in current application programming, allowing you to search for a specific pattern of characters inside a given string.

In the next chapter, you will see PHP and MySQL working together and learn how to create MySQL databases, tables, and use PHP programming code to handle them.

CHAPTER 10

PHP and MySQL Working Together

As you have seen so far, PHP is very capable and easy to manipulate and use to display data. Where does this data come from? There are two types of data that PHP can use: static and dynamic. We can think of static data as non-changing and dynamic as able-to-be-changed. This dynamic data is stored in a database. Simply put, a database is a structured organization of data. Think of a folder of spreadsheets. The key to databases, however, is that we can easily search or query a database based on how we have set up our structure. These queries can be as basic as "show me all the users' first names" to "show me all the first names of users who registered on a Tuesday after 2 p.m." The query complexity comes from the SQL in MySQL (Structured Query Language). This language, once understood, can be used with a Mad Libs approach in PHP. We can simply replace certain words and phrases with PHP variables in order to dynamically influence the result of the query.

In this chapter, we will start with the basics, of course, and simply get PHP to communicate with MySQL.

This chapter consists of the following sections:

- PHP Communication with MySQL

- MySQLi Advantages

- PHP Connection to a Database

© Gunnard Engebreth, Satej Kumar Sahu 2023
G. Engebreth and S. K. Sahu, *PHP 8 Basics*, https://doi.org/10.1007/978-1-4842-8082-9_10

PHP Communication with MySQL

As you saw before, PHP needs a web server in order to run on the Web. The same is needed for MySQL. A database server (DB) is needed to run and maintain the database. In your Docker dev environment, you have this already running. With Docker, you can type docker ps at any point on your host machine (the real physical machine you are using) to see what Docker containers you have running, as shown in Figure 10-1.

Figure 10-1. *Docker containers running*

On the top line is an IMAGE for mysql:8.0 and on the very right side is the name mysql-db. In order for PHP to use MySQL, you need to connect to it first. PHP comes with two different methods: through the MySQLi and PDO APIs. Below are code examples of each method.

PHP Communication with the MySQLi Method

```
<code>
<?php
// mysqli
$mysqli = new mysqli("mydomain", "user", "password",
"database");
$result = $mysqli->query("SELECT 'message' AS theMessage FROM
'messages'");
$row = $result->fetch_assoc();
echo $row['theMessage'];

</code>
```

Without getting into detail, right now at least, in the context of these examples, let's at least break them down and see what you are doing and why.

In this first MySQLi example, there should be some standout items that are recognizable on first read.

```
<code>
$mysqli = new mysqli("db.mysite.com", "user", "password",
"database");
</code>
```

You have $mysqli, which is a PHP variable being set to new mysqli with some parameters. You can gather from this that mysqli is a class and $mysqli will become an object once created. Let's see if you can determine what the parameters of the class constructor are without Googling for an answer. The first parameter is "db.mysite.com". The db in the subdomain stands for database so a logical guess would be that this first parameter is the database server. The next ones are straightforward: "user" is the username and "password" is the password for the user you are connecting with through PHP. The final parameter of "database" is, well... the name of the database. These four parameters are needed in order to create a valid MySQLi connection. They can be directly input, as in this example, or you can use variables such as $dbServer, $dbUser, $dbPass, and $dbName and store them in a separate file for your own organization. This will often be the case in PHP applications.

The next line is

```
$result = $mysqli->query("SELECT 'message' AS theMessage FROM
'messages'");
```

This sets $result equal to the result of the query method of the $mysqli object. You see this in the form of the syntax $mysqli->query. The properties that are passed make up the actual query you would like to send to MySQL. More on these queries later.

195

The next line is

```
$row = $result->fetch_assoc();
```

This sets the variable $row to the value of the object $result after the fetch_assoc() method is run. After the query, you can receive your results all at once or row by row from the server. To save resources on your server, you want all of the data at one time. This will allow you to use PHP to consume and parse the data however you please without bothering the database server more than you need to. The method fetch_assoc() is in a group of available methods for MySQL. These methods are

- mysqli_fetch_assoc() fetches a result row as an associative array.

- mysqli_fetch_array() fetches a result row as an associative array, a numeric array, or both.

- mysqli_fetch_row() gets a result row as an enumerated array.

- mysqli_fetch_object() returns the current row of a result set as an object.

In your example, $row is an array with associative values or key values for the array. This is different from a traditional array with numbered keys:

```
$row['firstname'] Vs $row[0]
```

firstname is the associative key value used to associate with the database column firstname. Now you have the variable $row set to the row or rows containing the data that you queried from the database.

The next line is

```
echo $row['_message'];
```

Here you use echo to show the results of the PHP function htmlentities on the variable $row, specifically the data in the ['_message'] id of the array. This is the specific data you are querying for.

PHP Communication with the PDO Method

Let's see how the PDO version of this differs.

```
<code>
<?php

// PDO
$pdo = new PDO('mysql:host=localhost;dbname=myDatabase, 'user',
'password');
$statement = $pdo->query("SELECT 'message' AS theMessage FROM
'messages'");
$row = $statement->fetch(PDO::FETCH_ASSOC);
echo $row['theMessage'];

</code>
```

The first line is

```
$pdo = new PDO('mysql:host=localhost;dbname=myDatabase, 'user',
'password');
```

Here you create a new object named $pdo from the class PDO with a similar structure for passing the database host, database name, username, and password to the constructor.

The next line is

```
$statement = $pdo->query("SELECT 'message' AS theMessage FROM
'messages'");
```

Here you set the $statement in a similar way to the $pdo object method query.

The next line is

$row = $statement->fetch(PDO::FETCH_ASSOC);

In a similar fashion to MySQLi, the data is fetched to an associative array.

The last line is

```
echo $row['_message'];
```

It simply outputs the resulting data from the database.

So now that you know how to connect to MySQL TWO different ways, which one do you use?

There *really* is not that much of a difference in performance between these two ways. PHP.net's documentation says "The impact is as low as 0.1%." Here are some key advantages between MySQLi and PDO.

MySQLi Advantages

- Asynchronous queries
- Ability to get more info on affected rows
- Proper database closing method
- Multiple queries at once
- Automatic cleanup with persistent connections

PDO Advantages

- Useful fetch modes
- Allowed to pass variables and values directly in to execute
- Ability to auto-detect variable types

- Option for automatically buffered results with prepared statements

- Named parameters

The real difference comes when using a database system outside of MySQL or mariaDB. PDO supports 12 database types and MySQLi only deals in MySQL-specific functionality. Since you are using MySQL 8.0 and only want to use those functions, you are using MySQLi.

PHP Connection to a Database

Let's go ahead and create a connection and test your database. First, let's go to `http://localhost/chapter4/seedDB.php`.

Do you see the following?

Warning   mysqli::__construct(): (HY000/2002): No such file or directory in **/var/www/chapter4/seedDB.php** on line **4**

```
Fatal error: Uncaught Error: mysqli object is already closed
in /var/www/chapter4/seedDB.php:6 Stack trace: #0 /var/www/
chapter4/seedDB.php(6): mysqli->query('Select * from u...') #1
{main} thrown in /var/www/chapter4/seedDB.php on line 6
```

Hmm, something must not be configured correctly. This is saying that there is an issue on line 4 of seedDB.php. Let's go take a look.

```
<code>
<?php

require_once('db.php');
$mysqli = new mysqli($DB_HOST, $DB_USER, $DB_PASS, $DB_
DATABASE);
</code>
```

Line 4 is the $mysqli = new mysqli line. This looks correct to me, so there must be an issue with the variables used in the mysqli constructor. As you see on line 3, you are reading these variables from db.php. Let's open that file.

```
<code>
<?php
$DB_HOST = '';
$DB_USER = 'root';
$DB_PASS = 'pass';
$DB_DATABASE = 'beginningPHP';

</code>
```

Ahh! Look at that! In line 2, $DB_HOST is set to "and not an actual host. If you remember, your host is set to db. Let's go ahead and replace the empty space with db.

```
<code>
<?php
$DB_HOST = 'db';
$DB_USER = 'root';
$DB_PASS = 'pass';
$DB_DATABASE = 'beginningPHP';
</code>
```

Ok. If you save this and reload http://localhost/chapter4/seedDB. php, you should see some better results.

```
<code>
Creating table "USERS"Seeing Users into table..1..2..3
Users added
1 - tom - hanks - 2021-06-25 17:58:42
2 - billy - mitchell - 2021-06-25 17:58:42
```

```
3 - mega - man - 2021-06-25 17:58:42
</code>
```

When you are developing applications, it is good to have some dummy data on hand in order to test your code appropriately. The act of taking data (dummy or actual from production) and populating a database with it is called *seeding*. Here you are seeding the database beginningPGP, specifically the table users, with three rows of user information. In this case, you are using a simple .sql file with the data. In larger frameworks like Laravel, this is done through migrations and a program called artisan. This allows for you not only to seed the database with data, but for your development team to stay on the same page with your data by allowing these migrations to be accessed like you would access your code in git (version control). Once you have run this page, press refresh. What happens? The code checks first to see if the table exists and does not seed it with user information if it already exists. Let's write some code that will show the users from this table.

Open showUsers.php in the chapter4 folder.

```
<code>
<?php
require_once('db.php');

$mysqli = new mysqli($DB_HOST, $DB_USER, $DB_PASS, $DB_
DATABASE);
$query = "SELECT * FROM users";

$result = $mysqli->query($query);
if ($result) {
    echo '<h1>Users in Database</h1>';
    while ($row = $result->fetch_assoc()) {
        echo "Name: {$row['first_name']} {$row['last_name']} =
        Created: {$row['created']} </br>";
```

```
    }
} else {
    echo "No Results. Have you run <a href='http://localhost/
    chapter4/seedDB.php'>SeedDB</a>?";
}
</code>
```

Let's go through this line by line.

```
<code>
<?php
require_once('db.php');
</code>
```

This is the standard beginning of a PHP file. You first require the db. php file to be loaded. Remember, this sets the variables for your database host, user, password, and database name.

```
<code>
$mysqli = new mysqli($DB_HOST, $DB_USER, $DB_PASS, $DB_
DATABASE);
$query = "SELECT * FROM users";
</code>
```

```
<code>
$result = $mysqli->query($query);
</code>
```

Here you use the object $mysqli and its method query to submit your query to the database. The result will be set as the variable $result.

```
<code>
if ($result) {
    echo '<h1>Users in Database</h1>';
    while ($row = $result->fetch_assoc()) {
```

```
    echo "Name: {$row['first_name']} {$row['last_name']} =
    Created: {$row['created']} </br>";
    }
} else {
    echo "No Results. Have you run <a href='http://localhost/
    chapter4/seedDB.php'>SeedDB</a>?";
}
</code>
```

This code may look complex but you are doing some pretty basic (for humans) logic. In programming languages, this type of "obvious to humans" logic takes precise logic handling in order to make sure that you account for all situations and stay away from errors. The `if ($result)` is PHP checking if $result evaluates to any "truthy" value. This can be

- Boolean TRUE
- Non-empty value
- Non-NULL value
- Non-zero number

You are basically asking if any useful data was found and returned to you. You will handle the scenario of nothing being returned a few lines down. First, let's deal with the data you do have.

```
<code>
 echo '<h1>Users in Database</h1>';
    while ($row = $result->fetch_assoc()) {
        echo "Name: {$row['first_name']} {$row['last_name']} =
        Created: {$row['created']} </br>";
    }
</code>
```

Here you echo out a header for the page using the HTML <h1> tags. Then you begin a while loop, which in PHP loop from beginning to end until a specified condition is meet. You can think of this like "while the traffic light is green, keep driving" or "while the pasta is not cooked, keep cooking." Once either of those two conditions change (the traffic light becomes red or the pasta is cooked), the loop will stop. In your code, you are saying "while $row is equal to data fetched from the database as an associative array, run the loop." Your loop is simple and it echoes your results from the database one row at a time. Once $row does not equal data from the database or the database is finished returning data, this loop will stop.

```
<code>
} else {
    echo "No Results. Have you run <a href='http://localhost/
    chapter4/seedDB.php'>SeedDB</a>?";
}
</code>
```

This else corresponds to the if ($results) from above. This is what happens if $result comes back empty. When this happens, you want to return some kind of useful error to the user and not just standard MySQL or PHP errors. These types of errors can be used against you by attackers. Here you echo to the user that perhaps the database is empty and they may need to run the seedDB file you ran earlier in order to put data into the database.

Here you see the use of MySQLi (as opposed to PDO) to connect PHP to the database, resulting in a database object named $mysqli. You want to select everything from the users table in your database so you use the query SELECT * FROM users. SELECT tells MySQL that you are requesting data. The * means everything. FROM tells MySQL where you want to get this data from, which is expected to be given as the next term. Finally, users is the table you want to get the data from. This is one of the most general queries you can do in MySQL. Let's modify this a bit. What if you want to retrieve the list of names in alphabetical order by last name? Modify the query and run this:

```
<code>
$query = "SELECT * FROM users ORDER by last_name ASC"
</code>
```

This code is also found in showUsers2.php.

This query looks very similar to the first one but with some modifiers. After users you add ORDER, which tells MySQL that you would like to have your data returned in an ordered fashion. At this point, you have not told MySQL anything else. You need two factors for MySQL to be able to order these results. First, you need to tell MySQL which column of data you would like to have ordered. Currently, you have id, first_name, last_name, and created. In your query, you have ORDERED by last_name, which satisfies this first requirement, but now you need to tell MySQL which order. There are two main options: ascending (ASC) or descending (DESC). Ascending, when dealing with strings like last names, is A-Z because the numeric value for a is smaller than z so this is considered to be ascending. The reverse is DESC, which would be Z-A. If you run this code now, you should see this output:

```
<code>
Users in Database
Name: tom hanks = Created: 2021-06-28 14:17:45
Name: mega man = Created: 2021-06-28 14:17:45
Name: billy mitchell = Created: 2021-06-28 14:17:45
</code>
```

Another useful modifier for this query is LIMIT. Let's say, for example, there are thousands of users in this database but you only want the top three ordered by score. This query would look like the following (also found in showUSers3.php):

```
<code>
$query = "SELECT * FROM users ORDER by score DESC LIMIT 3";
</code>
```

So far you have read from the database through the SELECT query. The purpose of using a database in the backend of your website is for data to both read and store data. This is how photos show up on Instagram and how tweets enter the twitterverse. A user can take their tweet (data) and send it to the database where it gets stored in a table with specific values assigned to the associated columns. Let's add another user to your database and you will see how this works. You will use PHP MySQL prepared statements. The advantage to using prepared statements is twofold:

1) Over iterations of queries, there is reduced parsing time even though the query is run more than once, so the result is that the queries are executed with high efficiency.

2) PHP MySQL prepared statements can be very useful against SQL injections.

Open up addUser.php and let's break it down.

```
<code>
<?php

require_once('db.php');
$mysqli = new mysqli($DB_HOST, $DB_USER, $DB_PASS, $DB_DATABASE);

$query = $mysqli->prepare("INSERT INTO users (first_name, last_name, age, score) values (?,?,?,?)");

$query->bind_param("ssii",$firstName, $lastName, $age, $score);
```

```
$firstName = "Freddy";
$lastName = "Krueger";
$age = 40;
$score = 301;

$query->execute();
$mysqli->close();
</code>
```

The first few lines should look familiar at this point. This is where you introduce the database variables stored in db.php and create an object named $mysqli from the mysqli class.

```
<code>
$query = $mysqli->prepare("INSERT INTO users (first_name, last_
name, age, score) values (?,?,?,?)");
</code>
```

This line looks familiar but very different. This is your INSERT query, which you are creating for use as a prepared statement.

```
<code>
$query = $mysqli->prepare
</code>
```

Here you create a variable named $query, which is the result of the method prepare from the object $mysqli. prepare takes the query you want to run in MySQL but gives you the ability to bind parameters to minimize bandwidth on the server, as you only send the parameters each time and not the whole query. The query uses the verb INSERT, which has a structure of

```
<code>
INSERT INTO <table> (column1, column2, column3, ...) VALUES
(Value1, value2, value3, ...);
</code>
```

You use the column structure of the users table to insert values for first_name, last_name, age, and score. But where are the values? There are only question marks (?s). This is the binding element. MySQL looks at these question marks and sets that space aside for the specified amount of values to be assigned later; in your code, it is on the next line.

```
<code>
$query->bind_param("ssii",$firstName, $lastName, $age, $score);
</code>
```

This code uses the $query object you created earlier and this time you use the bind_param method, which takes in two sets of parameters. The first ("ssii") in your example is the list of the types of parameters that you are binding. You are using "ssii", which stands for "string, string, integer, integer" or first_name, last_name, age, score. MySQL accepts four types:

- i: integer (i.e., 1, 199, 4421)

- d: double (1.0e6 to represent one million)

- s: string ("pants", "Bananas")

- b: BLOB (a binary large object is a varying-length binary string that can be up to 2,147,483,647 characters long)

Now that you have told MySQL what types of variables to expect, you list the variables you will be using.

```
<code>
$firstName = "Freddy";
$lastName = "Krueger";
$age = 40;
$score = 301;
</code>
```

Now you assign values to the variables you have already told MySQL you will be using for the query: two strings and two integers, just like you declared using "ssii".

```
<code>
$query->execute();
$mysqli->close();
</code>
```

Lastly, you execute the query by calling the method execute from the $query object and then you close the connection to MySQL.

Go to http://localhost/chapter4/addUser.php and then back to http://localhost/chapter4/showUser.php to see the results. You should see one additional user in the table. If you refresh addUser multiple times, you will get multiple additions to the table. Now that you have some basic techniques for interacting with MySQL, in the next chapter you will take a deeper dive into more complex queries, data organization, and MySQL features.

Summary

In this chapter, you learned the basics of working with PHP and MySQL. You first learned how to connect to the DB using two methods such as MySQLi and PDO. You learned the advantages of using one method or the other. Finally, you explored the code needed to connect to the DB and show the users included in it.

In the next chapter, you will learn more about the data types you can utilize in the MySQL DB table, like CHAR and VARCHAR, and how to define multiple dependencies in queries.

CHAPTER 11

Data

So far, you have used MySQL to store a simple user table with a few columns. This was good for some quick examples, but what about more complex queries that have multiple dependencies?

In this chapter, let's chart out some data that you can use for a camp registration/management database.

This chapter consists of the following sections.

- Planning for a New Database
- Creation of a New Database

Planning for a New Database

Databases work best when they are well organized with data and tables taken into consideration. Here are a few things to consider when planning your database:

1)   Always use the proper datatype.
One of the main MySQL best practices is to utilize datatypes dependent on the idea or inherent nature of the information. Utilizing unessential datatypes may eat up more space or lead to mistakes.

For instance, using VARCHAR (20) rather than a DATETIME datatype for storing date-time values will prompt mistakes in date-time–related computations. Additionally, it is conceivable that invalid information will be thrown into the mix, ultimately causing mistakes.

© Gunnard Engebreth, Satej Kumar Sahu 2023
G. Engebreth and S. K. Sahu, *PHP 8 Basics*, https://doi.org/10.1007/978-1-4842-8082-9_11

2) Use CHAR (1) over VARCHAR (1).

VARCHAR (1) takes additional bytes to store data, so assuming your string is a single character, it is better to utilize CHAR (1).

3) Utilize the CHAR datatype to store just fixed length information.

For instance, if the length of the information is under 1,000, utilizing single (1000) rather than VARCHAR (1000) will devour more space.

4) Try not to use provincial date designs.

When using DATETIME or DATE datatypes, consistently use the YYYY-MM-DD date arrangement or ISO date design reasonable for your SQL Engine. Territorial organizations like DD-MM-YYYY or MM-DD-YYYY will not be stored properly and will result in errors and frustration.

5) List key sections.

It is beneficial that the inquiry returns the outcome quickly, so record the sections that are utilized in JOIN conditions.

On the off chance that you use the UPDATE proclamation including more than one table, file every one of the sections that are utilized to join the tables.

6) Do not use functions over indexed columns.

This is the purpose of an index. By trying to replicate the indexing process through the use of functions, you are overcomplicating the situation and therefore slowing the whole process down.

For instance, say you need to get information where the initial two characters of the camper are GE. You use the following:

```
SELECT firstname FROM campers WHERE firstname like 'GE%'
```

Furthermore, don't write

```
SELECT firstname FROM campers WHERE left (firstname,2)='GE'
```

The first example makes use of the index, which results in a faster response time.

7)   Use ORDER BY clauses only if needed.

Let the PHP order your data, not MySQL. With MySQL, you can set an order for the data to be returned by, like ASC for ascending or DESC for descending. This can result in your queries taking additional time that PHP or even JavaScript on your front end can do.

8)   Choose a proper database engine.

If you develop an application that reads data more often than writes it (e.g., a search engine), choose a MyISAM storage engine.

Choosing the wrong storage engine will affect the performance. The storage engines available to you are MyISAM, which is the default MySQL storage engine, or InnoDB, which is an alternative engine built into MySQL and intended for high-performance databases. One of the main differences between these two is table locking vs. row-level locking. Table locking is the technique of locking an entire table when one or more cells within the table need to be updated or deleted. Table locking is the default method employed by the default storage engine, MyISAM. Row-level locking is the act of locking an effective range of rows in a table while one or more cells within the range are modified or deleted. Row-level locking is the method used by the InnoDB storage engine and is intended for high-performance databases.

9)   Use the EXISTS clause wherever needed.

When you need to only check if the data exists, use the MySQL EXISTS function instead of initiating an entire query in order to evaluate the return data. For example, use

```
If EXISTS(SELECT * from Table WHERE col='foo')
```

Do not use

```
If (SELECT count(*) from Table WHERE col='foo')>0
```

10)   EXPLAIN your SELECT queries.

MySQL comes with the ability to EXPLAIN a query in terms of how MySQL executes the process, such as

```
mysql> EXPLAIN ANALYZE SELECT * FROM SALES;
+----------------------------------------------------+
| EXPLAIN                                            |
+----------------------------------------------------+
| -> Table scan on SALES (cost=0.35 rows=1) (actual  |
| time=0.070..0.070 rows=0 loops=1)                  |
+----------------------------------------------------+
1 row in set (4.15 sec)
```

Creation of a New Database

With all you've learned so far, let's create your new database with the following structure:

> **Table Name:** Campers
>
> **Columns:** ID, First Name, Last Name, Age, Camp ID, Created
>
> **Table Name:** Camps
>
> **Columns:** ID, Name, Size, Created
>
> **Table Name:** Registered
>
> **Columns:** ID, Camper ID, Camp ID, Registered, Paid, Created

This is a basic design for a database that a camp would use in order to keep track of their campers, camp sites, and registrations. In order to use this properly for your project, you need to set up and create these tables, seed them with data, and use PHP to manage them through table relationships. While there are several front-end GUI methods of managing MySQL, you will not be using any of them for now. We will take you through these next steps via the command-line interface (or CLI) of MySQL. First, get to a command prompt (Windows) or terminal (Mac OS, Linux) and run

```
<code>
docker ps
</code>
```

Remember this command? This shows all the running containers. If nothing shows up, you may not be running Docker for this book. Please go back to the first chapter of this book and make sure you have Docker running and docker-compose up has been run.

If everything is running properly, you should see something similar to this:

```
docker ps
CONTAINER ID    IMAGE                        COMMAND
CREATED            STATUS
PORTS                                                  NAMES
d5d98b7de503    beginning-php8-and-mysql_app    "docker-php-entrypoi..."
2 days ago         Up 2 days
9000/tcp                                               php-app
63715c3c4f52    nginx:alpine                 "/docker-entrypoint...."
2 days ago         Up 2 days
0.0.0.0:80->80/tcp, :::80->80/tcp                      php-nginx
21f2a4b87b7b    mysql:8.0                    "docker-entrypoint.s..."
2 days ago         Up 2 days
0.0.0.0:3306->3306/tcp, :::3306->3306/tcp, 33060/tcp    mysql-db
```

You can see that your MySQL container is named mysql-db and with Docker you can now connect to that container just like you would to a server.

```
<code>
docker exec -ti mysql-db bash
</code>
```

This command tells Docker that you would like to execute a command named -ti to create a pseudo TTYl. This basically allows you to use your terminal to be the interface to this container while the i stands for interactive mode, meaning you want to use this container like a live system. The next attribute is mysql-db, which is the name of the container you are connecting to, and finally you want to run bash. Bash is a shell for Unix/Linux systems that allows you access to the filesystem and to run scripts. Once you press Enter, you will be "inside" the My SQL container. Once connected, you need to run the following:

```
<code>
mysql -uroot -ppass
</code>
```

This connects you to MySQL using the username root and password pass. This is typically not encouraged, but in closed networking situations and development environments you can allow for such casualness.

The first thing you need to know and do once connected to MySQL is list the databases.

```
<code>
show databases;
</code>
```

Note that all MySQL commands end with a semicolon. If you type a command and press Enter without the semicolon, it will just move down to the next line and wait for you to type more or to type a semicolon. You can just type a semicolon and then Enter to continue with your command.

In this list, you should see beginningPHP. Type

```
<code>
use beginningPHP;
</code>
Now type

<code>
show tables;
</code>
```

This command, well, shows the tables available in the current database you are using. There should be a users table. This is fine and you will just set it aside for now. Let's begin creating the tables for your camping data.

In the chapter5 directory there is a file called campers.sql.

```
<code>
create table IF NOT EXISTS campers(
        id INT NOT NULL AUTO_INCREMENT,
        first_name VARCHAR(100) NOT NULL,
        last_name VARCHAR(40) NOT NULL,
        age INT NOT NULL,
    campId INT default 0,
        created DATETIME NOT NULL ON UPDATE CURRENT_
        TIMESTAMP default current_timestamp,
        PRIMARY KEY ( id )
);
</code>
```

Take this code and paste it into the MySQL command line and press Enter. Now type show tables; again.

```
<code>
mysql> show tables;
+------------------------+
| Tables_in_beginningPHP |
+------------------------+
| campers                |
| users                  |
+------------------------+
2 rows in set (0.00 sec)
</code>
```

You now have a `campers` table in the database. To see the structure of a table, type

```
<code>
desc campers;
</code>
```

`Desc` is for Describe and it will show you the layout for the table. Now let's create the table to hold the information for your camps. Look inside `camps.sql` in the `chapter5` directory.

```
<code>
create table IF NOT EXISTS camps(
        id INT NOT NULL AUTO_INCREMENT,
        camp_name VARCHAR(100) NOT NULL,
        size INT NOT NULL,
        created DATETIME NOT NULL ON UPDATE CURRENT_
        TIMESTAMP default current_timestamp,
        PRIMARY KEY ( id )
);
</code>
```

Copy and paste this code into the MySQL command line and press Enter.

Now type show tables; and see the results:

```
<code>
show tables;
+------------------------+
| Tables_in_beginningPHP |
+------------------------+
| campers                |
| camps                  |
+------------------------+
2 rows in set (0.03 sec)
</code>
```

Lastly, let's create a table for the registered campers. Repeat the steps from above with registered.sql.

Open registered.sql. Copy and paste the code into the MySQL command line and press Enter.

Type show tables; and see the results.

Now that you have your data, let's see next how you can use relational queries to create simple and complex queries for your app.

Summary

In this chapter, you learned which data types you can utilize in a MySQL DB table, like CHAR or VARCHAR, and how to define multiple dependencies in queries.

In the next chapter, you will combine everything you have learned into one example website to create, read, update, and delete data (otherwise known as CRUD). You will learn how a basic CRUD website can be a standard way to manage information within a business or organization.

CHAPTER 12

Website with a DB

In this chapter, you will be combining everything you have learned into one example website. This website will allow you to create, read, update, and delete (otherwise known as CRUD). A basic CRUD website is a standard way to manage information within a business or organization. Almost every application out there can be broken down into CRUD if you think about it. Facebook allows you to create posts, read posts, update them or your profile, and delete information. This functionality is the basic interaction that most websites are looking for, but your imagination is the limit to where you can go with it.

This chapter will cover the following:

- The PHP CRUD `GET` method and example functions: `deleteBook`, `showEditBook`, `showAddBook`, and `showBooks`

- The PHP CRUD `POST` method for examples `bookToUpdate` and `bookToAdd`

For this example, you will create the basic CRUD for you to review and add to. This CRUD uses both `POST` and `GET` methods as well as MySQL PDO parameter binding. This is a great first step towards developing a more dynamic and advanced application.

Let's get right into this with `home.php` within the chapter12 link.

```php
<?php
$title = "Home";
$thisDir = 12;
?>
```

© Gunnard Engebreth, Satej Kumar Sahu 2023
G. Engebreth and S. K. Sahu, *PHP 8 Basics*, https://doi.org/10.1007/978-1-4842-8082-9_12

These first lines declare some global variables.

```
<!DOCTYPE html>
<html lang="en">
<head>
<link href="../bootstrap/css/bootstrap.min.css"
rel="stylesheet">
</head>
<div class="container">
    <header class="d-flex flex-wrap justify-content-center
    py-3 mb-4 border-bottom">
      <a href="/" class="d-flex align-items-center mb-3 mb-
      md-0 me-md-auto text-dark text-decoration-none">
        <svg class="bi me-2" width="40" height="32"><use
        xlink:href="#bootstrap"></use></svg>
        <span class="fs-4"><?= $title ?></span>
      </a>

      <ul class="nav nav-pills">
    <li class="nav-item"><a href="home.php" class="nav-link"
    aria-current="page">Home</a></li>
    <li class="nav-item"><a href="home.php?q=add" class="nav-
    link" aria-current="page">Add</a></li>
      </ul>
    </header>
<div>

</div>
```

This section creates the header and navigation for the app. For now, these links are static, but they can be made dynamic through reading menu items from a database, for example.

```php
<?php
try {
    echo '<br />';
    echo 'Current PHP version: ' . phpversion();
    echo '<br />';

    $host = 'mysql-db';
    $dbname = 'beginningPHP';
    $user = 'user';
    $pass = 'pass';
    $dsn = "mysql:host=$host;dbname=$dbname;charset=utf8";
    $conn = new PDO($dsn, $user, $pass);

    echo 'Database connected successfully';
    echo '<br />';
} catch (\Throwable $t) {
    echo 'Error: ' . $t->getMessage();
    echo '<br />';
}
```

This is your basic database connection block. Here you attempt to connect with your credentials and return an error if there are any issues. You will use the $conn variable next in several functions. You will need to use global $conn within those functions because this variable exists outside the scope of the new functions.

```php
function deleteBook($theBook) {
    global $conn;
    $sql = "delete FROM `books` WHERE `id`=$theBook";
    $result = $conn->query($sql);
    echo "Book Deleted<br />";
}
```

This function deleteBook takes the passed-in variable $theBook and targets the database item through a specific database query. The function then returns "Book Deleted." This function can be improved in multiple ways:

- Variable sanitization to protect against SQL injection attacks

- Verification that the item to delete exits

- Checking for MySQL errors and showing them

```
function showEditBook($theBook) {
    global $conn;
    $sql = "SELECT * FROM `books` WHERE `id`=$theBook";
    $result = $conn->query($sql);
    foreach($result as $row) {
        $addForm ='<form action="home.php"
        method="post"><table>';
        $addForm .= '<tr><td>Title</td><td><input type="text"
        name="title" value="'.$row['title'].'"></td></tr>';
        $addForm .= '<tr><td>Author</td><td><input type="text"
        name="author" value="'.$row['author'].'"></td></tr>';
        $addForm .= '<tr><td>Category</
        td><td><input type="text" name="category"
        value="'.$row['category'].'"></td></tr>';
        $addForm .= '<tr><td>ISBN</td><td><input type="text"
        name="isbn" value="'.$row['isbn'].'"></td></tr>';
        $addForm .= '<tr><td></td><td><input type="submit"
        name="submit"></td></tr>';
```

```
        $addForm .= '<input type="hidden" name="bookToUpdate"
        value="'.$row['id'].'">';
        $addForm .= '</table></form>';
        echo $addForm;
    }
}
```

The function showEditBook shows the edit book form given the book id ($theBook). With this form, you then submit it back to home.php via POST. With this form, you can add validation to ensure that values are properly filled out and able to be added into the database. The hidden field is there as an indicator to home.php as to how to handle the form submission. You will get to that later when you update the book in a function.

```
function showAddBook() {
    $addForm ='<form action="home.php" method="post"><table>';
    $addForm .= '<tr><td>Title</td><td><input type="text"
    name="title"></td></tr>';
    $addForm .= '<tr><td>Author</td><td><input type="text"
    name="author"></td></tr>';
    $addForm .= '<tr><td>Category</td><td><input type="text"
    name="category"></td></tr>';
    $addForm .= '<tr><td>ISBN</td><td><input type="text"
    name="isbn"></td></tr>';
    $addForm .= '<tr><td></td><td><input type="submit"
    name="submit"></td></tr>';
    $addForm .= '<input type="hidden" name="bookToAdd"
    value="true">';
    $addForm .= '</table></form>';
    echo $addForm;
}
```

The function showAddBook shows the Add a book form. Again, here you use a hidden field to notify home.php via POST what action you want to take.

```php
function showBooks() {
    global $conn;
    $sql = "SELECT * FROM `books` WHERE `id`";
    $result = $conn->query($sql);
    if ($result !== false) {
        $rowCount = $result->rowCount();
        echo "Number of Books: $rowCount <br />";
    }
    foreach($result as $row) {
        echo $row['id'].' - '. $row['title'] .' - '.
        $row['author'] .' - '. $row['category'] .' - '.
        $row['isbn'] .'  [ <a href="home.php?q=edit&book='.$row
        ['id'].'"> Edit</a> <a href="home.php?q=delete&book='.$
        row['id'].'"> Delete</a> ]<br />';
    }
}
```

The function showBooks is the default display of the page. It shows all of the books in the database with links to edit and delete.

```php
if (isset($_GET['q'])) {
    if ($_GET['q'] == 'add') {
        echo "Adding Book<br />";
        showAddBook();
    }
    if ($_GET['q'] == 'edit') {
        $theBook = $_GET['book'];
        echo "Editing Book<br />";
        showEditBook($theBook);
    }
```

```php
    if ($_GET['q'] == 'delete') {
        $theBook = $_GET['book'];
        echo "Deleting Book<br />";
        deleteBook($theBook);
    }
}
```

Above is the logic that you use to determine what action to take via GET. Remember that GET variables are the ones used within the URL. You use q as the variable you assign to the action (add, edit, delete) in your URL.

```php
if (isset($_POST['bookToUpdate'])) {
    global $conn;
    $sql = "update books set title=?, author=?, category=?,
    isbn=? where id=?";
    if ($stmt = $conn->prepare($sql)) {
        $stmt->bindParam(1,$_POST['title']);
        $stmt->bindParam(2,$_POST['author']);
        $stmt->bindParam(3,$_POST['category']);
        $stmt->bindParam(4,$_POST['isbn']);
        $stmt->bindParam(5,$_POST['bookToUpdate']);
        if($stmt->execute()) {
            echo "Book ". $_POST['title'] ."added";
        }
    } else {
        echo "Error: " . $sql . "<br>" . $conn->error;
        echo "</br>Stmt error: ".$stmt->error();
    }
}
```

The above if statement checks to see if you are calling for the variable bookToUpdate. If this variable is set, then you attempt to update a book.

You use the PDO, as explained in Chapter 10, to prepare a statement to ensure that you are protecting against SQL injections and to specify variables. Once $stmt is executed, you return the book title and "added;" otherwise, you return the error. This can be improved by

- Sanitizing POST data

- Verifying that the item in the DB is available to update

```
if (isset($_POST['bookToAdd'])) {
    global $conn;
    $sql = "insert into books (title, author, category, isbn)
    VALUES (?,?,?,?)";
    if ($stmt = $conn->prepare($sql)) {
        $stmt->bindParam(1,$_POST['title']);
        $stmt->bindParam(2,$_POST['author']);
        $stmt->bindParam(3,$_POST['category']);
        $stmt->bindParam(4,$_POST['isbn']);
        if($stmt->execute()) {
            echo "New Book added";
        }
    }
}
```

This if statement checks for the POST variable bookToAdd. If it is found, then the SQL query is created and executed. This can be improved by

- Sanitizing POST data

- Verifying that the item is not already in the DB

- All values are filled out

```
showBooks();
```

This is the default view for this page, a list of books available:

```
?>
  </div>
```

With the improvements listed above, try turning this into an API that returns JSON data. Instead of returning HTML, the output should look something like this pseudo-code:

```
$sql = "SELECT * FROM `books` WHERE `id`";
    $result = $conn->query($sql);
    if ($result !== false) {
        $rowCount = $result->rowCount();
        $output[] =  "Number of Books: $rowCount";
    }
    foreach($result as $row) {
        $output[] = "title:". $row['title'];
        $output[] = "author:". $row['author'];
        $output[] = "category:". $row['category'];
        $output[] = "isbn:". $row['isbn'];
        $output = json_encode($output);
        Return $output;
    }
```

Summary

In this chapter, you combined everything you have learned so far and build one example website. You learned how to build this website to create, read, update, and delete (otherwise known as CRUD) and use it with both POST and GET methods as well as the MySQL PDO parameter binding.

In the next chapter, you will learn about frameworks, which use a lot of best practices and design patterns so as to allow developers to quickly use them to solve problems.

CHAPTER 13

Introduction to Frameworks

After having learned in the previous chapters how to build a website, in this chapter you will focus on programming development frameworks. You will learn what they are and when to use them.

This chapter consists of the following sections:

- Introduction to Frameworks

- Pros and Cons of Frameworks

- MVC Pattern

- Different Layers of a Framework

- Different Types of Frameworks

- Introduction of PHP Standard Recommendation (PSR)

- PHP Frameworks

Introduction to Frameworks

Until now, you have built the different layers of an application: the UI components to parse values and display the view pages, connect to the database and fetch data, authenticate use, and maintain sessions. If you observe, these contextual areas are reusable structures and elements that are used in every project or application based on different use cases.

© Gunnard Engebreth, Satej Kumar Sahu 2023
G. Engebreth and S. K. Sahu, *PHP 8 Basics*, https://doi.org/10.1007/978-1-4842-8082-9_13

They have structural value but do not add value in terms of helping developers and teams develop new features and business logic. Recognizing the recurrence of these common structural elements, many smart people felt that they could be developed and packaged together so that these structures could interface with each other and be reused. In essence, they created a framework, which is a supporting structure that helps you get started developing your applications, thus delivering business value, instead of you spending time developing a session layer, a database connection layer, and then a security component.

Frameworks use a lot of best practices and design patterns to allow developers to quickly use them to solve problems.

With this said, should you build a framework for your own use case? This may not be necessary since all frameworks nowadays provide a way to install any packages you might need but are not present already within the framework. They also allow you to build custom layers by extending the framework or plugin systems. If they are open source, if a need arises, you can fork them and use the foundations of existing frameworks to build upon them.

Pros and Cons of Frameworks

Frameworks have a lot to offer, but they are not without drawbacks. In this section, you'll explore the pros and cons.

Pros of Using Frameworks

There are many benefits to using frameworks:

1. Speeds up application development

   Frameworks help you to focus on working on new features/requirements instead of building reusable patterns and testing the frameworks, authentication, and authorization processes. This saves a lot of time in terms of building the foundation of a secure, standard code base, which a framework provides.

2. Simplifies application maintenance

    With the core foundation being maintained by the framework team, it becomes easy for the development team to maintain the application features and upgrade the core framework from time to time.

3. Decoupled patterns

    Frameworks come preloaded with a variety of patterns, which resemble a decoupled system design like having a message queue abstraction on top of a variety of message queue platforms, thus providing state-of-the-art coding structures that otherwise would be need to be developed by developers.

4. Updated patches

    Frameworks are built and maintained by a lot of internal as well as community-based open source developers, QA engineers, and other smart people who take care of handling changes, upgrading packages, integrating new features as and when they become relevant, and patching security issues. Given the knowledge of such a community team, it becomes a piece of cake to get these changes just with a version upgrade.

5. Task automation

    Frameworks provide command-line tools to create base code for new features like a unit test case or a controller with a standard structure, which can then be modified by you for your application-specific requirements. This makes it very easy to quickly prototype and build components.

Cons of Using Frameworks

As alluded to earlier, frameworks do have some potential drawbacks:

1. Performance of the application is affected.

   Frameworks comprise a large amount of code for the base structure, which helps to quickly bootstrap your projects. On the other hand, there is a performance penalty since many components may not be applicable to your project but still are loaded during packaging and run time.

2. Lack of support or active development

   A framework may have an active current development cycle but things may change in the future. It's crucial to consider past and current patterns of the framework team, development, and activity.

3. Learning curve

   Learning frameworks is a fun and challenging task. Some frameworks are very intuitive while others require a lot of configuration before starting. With many base and advanced components and concepts, learning a framework takes time on the part of the development teams.

MVC Pattern

MVC stands for the Model, View, and Controller Pattern. It's a very handy and useful design pattern that many frameworks use for separation of concerns. In previous chapters, you divided your code into UI, routing, processing, and a business logic layer. Similarly, frameworks separate out code into these logical structures and allow integration and control flow between them through many standard, evolved, and secure practices.

As shown in Figure 13-1, when any request is received by a PHP server, it hits the controller, which is usually the routing layer responsible for defining the GET, POST, and other REST verb-based API endpoints. The controller functions for respective endpoints receive the request and then call the Model layer to fetch any data or run any business logic after fetching data from another service. After the controller receives this data, it sends it to the View layer, which contains your UI code and generates the dynamic UI based on the model data sent to it. Once the View layer is processed, this is sent as response back to the browser or user.

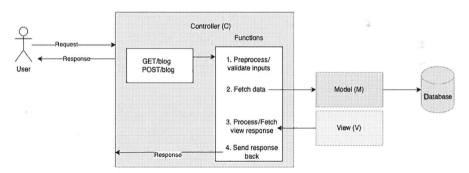

Figure 13-1. The Model-View-Controller architecture

Different Layers of a Framework

1. MVC layer

   All major frameworks use some variation of the MVC pattern as the core structural component to manage requests and control flow.

2. Dependency injection

   With many core components, like authentication/authorization/entity access, it becomes crucial to have a centralized logic to access these entities/components through dynamic injection rather than initializing them in each file where they are used, thus enabling reuse and manageability.

3. Authentication/authorization

   Authentication/authorization allows developers to validate users and also implement authorization through standard practices and in many cases also allow integration to Active Directory and other third-party services.

4. Session management

   Session management helps to validate users once they have logged in. In many cases, this is achieved through token-based authentication using JWT and other standards.

5. Database libraries

   Frameworks provide database libraries to connect to a variety of databases.

6. Test framework

   Frameworks also provide a test framework to write
   unit, functional, and integration tests. These tests
   help to mock and stub internal components, thus
   allowing developers to practice TDD-based design
   development.

7. Package management

   Composer is the central piece of library
   management, and it allows reusability of many
   standard libraries across frameworks, thus helping
   with interoperability among frameworks.

8. Other

   There are many other components like guard rails,
   message queue management, and caching, that are
   part of the core components.

Different Types of Frameworks

Let's quickly run through some of the different frameworks available to
PHP developers.

Based on use case:

1. REST API-based frameworks

   Many back-end applications nowadays just provide
   a RESTful interface that is accessed from a front-end
   application built on React or Angular or another front-
   end library or framework. So many frameworks provide
   an out-of-box solution to create REST API backends.

   Examples: Lumen, Silex, Slim, Guzzle, Symphony

2. FULLSTACK-based frameworks

These frameworks have some UI components integrated to allow you to develop UI code from within the platform.

Examples: Laravel, CakePHP, CodeIgniter, Laminas

Based on initial components packaged:

1. Micro frameworks:

These frameworks provide you with the bare minimum base to start, plus guidelines. These frameworks are very light. Based on your use case, you can choose different packages and design patterns. This will require some extra effort and knowledge on your part to build these patterns.

Example: Slim

2. Full-fledged frameworks

These frameworks come with all the fire power. In many cases, you may not need some of these packages but they are still included when deploying your application. The downside is the huge size of the framework, but it's helpful for teams to use the already established patterns and styles.

Example: Laravel

Role of Composer

With the emergence of many frameworks, there was a need to also have many third-party libraries for integration to different APIs. They can be integrated into frameworks through extensions and following framework-specific methodology. This can be quite cumbersome since it requires extensive knowledge of the inner workings of the framework plus the external API. In addition, you must handle the standards, best practices, and security while doing so. This is not the core responsibility of the developer. So, PHP introduced a package manager that can be used to install third-party packages and libraries that are created by community and third-party vendors. With it, developers can reuse these libraries and get updates as and when the source team publishes them. This helps in having a versioned library to be used across different frameworks.

Link: `https://getcomposer.org/`

Installing Composer is very easy. It just takes these few commands at `https://getcomposer.org/download/`.

All PHP frameworks use Composer for internal dependencies. As such, they come prepackaged with a Composer configuration, which can be extended.

When Composer is used, it creates a `composer.json` file that stores all the installed packages with their respective version in the JSON format.

Introduction of PHP Standard Recommendation (PSR)

With the emergence of so many PHP frameworks and the use of Composer for package management, to make the process easy for developers to use different frameworks and for interoperability, there needed to be a common standard on which all these frameworks should be based. This led to the creation of PHP Standard Recommendations (PSR), a PHP specification published by the PHP Framework Interoperability Group (PHP-FIG). It serves as the standardization of programming concepts in PHP.

The goal is to enable interoperability of components and packages. The PHP-FIG was established and formed by several PHP framework founders. The general idea is "moving PHP forward through collaboration and standards."

The full list of standards can be found at `www.php-fig.org/psr/#numerical-index`. Some are deprecated and some are in draft status. The current active ones can be found at `www.php-fig.org/psr/#index-by-status`.

Here are a few principle areas of PSRs:

1. Autoloading

    Autoloading helps load classes and libraries by resolving namespaces to their respective file system paths.

    Associated PSRs: PSR-4 Improved Autoloading

2. Interfaces

    Interfaces help in establishing contracts between shareable code structures.

    Associated PSRs:

    - PSR-3: Logger Interface

    - PSR-6: Caching Interface

    - PSR-11: Container Interface

    - PSR-13: Hypermedia Links

    - PSR-14: Event Dispatcher

    - PSR-16: Simple Cache

3. HTTP

    A standards-based approach to handle HTTP requests and responses

Associated PSRs:

- PSR-7: HTTP Message Interfaces

- PSR-15: HTTP Handlers

- PSR-17: HTTP Factories

- PSR-18: HTTP Client

4. Coding styles

   Coding standards to reduce cognitive friction and better readability

   Associated PSRs:

- PER Coding Style

- PSR-1: Basic Coding Standard

- PSR-12: Extended Coding Style Guide

PHP Frameworks

The following are a few popular and widely used PHP frameworks. You will use a few of them in later chapters.

- Laravel, `https://laravel.com/`

- Codeigniter, `www.codeigniter.com/`

- Symfony, `https://symfony.com/`

- Cakephp, `https://cakephp.org/`

- Laminas, `https://getlaminas.org/`

Choosing a Framework

With a plethora of frameworks available, it may be a bit confusing. How do you select the right one? Here are a few points to consider:

1. Application/business use case compatibility

   There are many use cases, and each application is unique in terms of its requirements. Some applications are more content-specific. For example, managing a blog for a team for which WordPress would be more suitable. In another case, a team may need to build a RESTful application for which Lumen or a similar framework may be helpful.

2. Developer skill set

   The core skill set of the development team also plays a principal role. If the team already knows a particular framework or design patterns particular to a framework, it's easy to reuse the existing skill set.

3. Learning curve

   Timelines of projects play a major role in terms of framework choice. Pick a framework that has a suitable learning curve so you can quickly start building your project.

4. Documentation

   Documentation plays a very important role. A framework without good documentation is like wandering in a forest without a map. Good documentation gives developers confidence to quickly experiment and follow up with a deep dive.

5. Testing framework

   A framework should be integrated with a test framework that can be used to write integration, functional, and unit tests. Many frameworks provide easy integration of tests and also help with mocking internal functionality of the framework so as to easily and quickly run unit tests.

6. Community support

   A community of internal, external, and open source commitment in terms of support and query answering in different forums like Stack Overflow is a very good indicator of people using it and being interested in answering questions related to problems they may have already faced, thus helping development teams gain confidence.

7. Active release/development

   A framework that is actively developed and has an active approach towards security and bug fixes on a regular basis gives confidence towards a future where this product will be supported on an ongoing basis.

8. Licenses

   It's very important to review the licenses of the framework related to its code sharing, editing, open source nature, and details relevant to production use.

9. Customization/extensibility

The ability of the framework to customize and extend core features to support unique extensions as per application requirements is very important.

10. Convention vs. customization

There is always a choice between convention and customization. Some frameworks are very particular about conventions and rules to be followed with the intention to reduce setup and help with a quick start on projects, while other frameworks choose a more open structure that can be customized as per your choice and application structure.

11. IDE support

With many popular IDEs nowadays, it becomes important to support the generation of code snippets through shortcuts instead of copy-and-paste to improve developer productivity.

12. Blogs/tutorials

Many frameworks provide their own internal blogs and tutorials to leverage the expertise of the core open community team. They also announce new resources, features, and use cases on an ongoing basis through news channels, announcements, and mailing chains.

13. Test coverage

It's important to validate that the core framework has full test coverage, which lays the importance of the core teams TDD-based development practices for the framework and also is an indicator of the quality of the core framework.

Summary

In this chapter, you learned why frameworks are an important part of the software development life cycle and make the life of developers easier and more fun by allowing them to reuse existing components of a framework to quickly start building new features and innovations. You explored why the choice of a framework is very important. It must be done by considering a variety of key points as well as the application to be built.

In the next chapter, you will focus on the Laravel PHP framework, which is a very popular web application framework that is easy to use and has an elegant syntax.

CHAPTER 14

Introduction to Laravel

Lately the development of web applications and websites has become more and more simple as developers make use of development tools. Let's explore which PHP framework can support web developers when building new web projects and applications.

In this chapter, you will focus on the Laravel PGP framework, which is a very popular web application framework that is easy to use and offers an elegant syntax. It helps you with common tasks such as a fast routing engine, real-time event broadcasting, database-agnostic schema migrations, and more.

This chapter consists of the following sections:

- Introduction to Laravel

- Installing Laravel

- Database Setup and Configuration

- Database Migrations

- Controller Route

- Registration View Form

- Storing User Data in a Database

© Gunnard Engebreth, Satej Kumar Sahu 2023
G. Engebreth and S. K. Sahu, *PHP 8 Basics*, https://doi.org/10.1007/978-1-4842-8082-9_14

Introduction to Laravel

Laravel is a modern PHP framework based on the MVC design pattern. An excerpt from the website explains it the best: *"Laravel is a web application framework with expressive, elegant syntax. We've already laid the foundation—freeing you to create without sweating the small things."*

Installing Laravel

There are many ways Laravel can be installed. They can be found at `https://laravel.com/docs/9.x/installation#your-first-laravel-project`.

You will be following the simplest one to get you up and running. Please make sure these prerequisites are installed before proceeding:

- PHP
- Composer

To start a new project with the name of blog-app, run the following command:

```
composer create-project laravel/laravel blog-app
```

The project structure looks like Figure 14-1 without the .git directory.

```
.editorconfig
.env
.env.example
.git/
.gitattributes
.gitignore
README.md
app/
artisan*
bootstrap/
composer.json
composer.lock
config/
database/
lang/
package.json
phpunit.xml
public/
resources/
routes/
storage/
tests/
vendor/
vite.config.js
```

Figure 14-1. *Laravel project directory structure*

Let's explore the common parts of the directory.

Once the project has been created, start it using the following commands:

```
cd blog-app
php artisan serve
```

You can now access the app at http://localhost:8000, as shown in Figure 14-2.

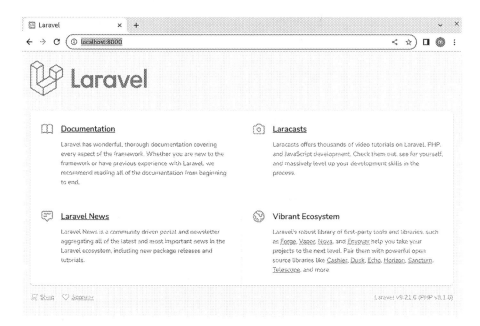

Figure 14-2. *Laravel main web page*

This should confirm a valid installation and setup of Laravel.

Database Setup and Configuration

You will learn about the various components of Laravel as you build one sub-part of your blog application, which is user registration. Along the way, you will see how Laravel makes it easy for you to build such an application.

The core of any application is data, and you will need a database to store data related to your users.

You will create the table in an incremental fashion as you proceed through the different steps. In previous chapters you created the database and tables manually, using the phpMyAdmin interface. This usually works for a demo project, but while working on a production project, it is suggested to maintain databases and tables in migrations, which are stored in files and can be committed to source code management systems like git.

This helps to have a repeatable data structure that can be readily used by other team members to get quickly onboarded and set up the project and also to create different environments for running projects like dev, staging, and production. An added benefit is having a versioned schema of your database and tables to understand and maintain the history of changes for auditing and other such purposes.

Before you start setting up the migration aspect of Laravel, you must configure the database configuration settings. They can be found in the file config/database.php. Let's review the contents of this file.

```
'default' => env('DB_CONNECTION', 'mysql'),
```

The default connection uses the mysql adapter, which suits your setup. Reviewing the connections section, you see the configs specific to the mysql connection.

```
'connections' => [

        'sqlite' => [

            ...

        ],

        'mysql' => [
            'driver' => 'mysql',
            'url' => env('DATABASE_URL'),
            'host' => env('DB_HOST', '127.0.0.1'),
            'port' => env('DB_PORT', '3306'),
            'database' => env('DB_DATABASE', ''),
            'username' => env('DB_USERNAME', 'root'),
            'password' => env('DB_PASSWORD', ),
            'unix_socket' => env('DB_SOCKET', ''),
            'charset' => 'utf8mb4',
```

```
            'collation' => 'utf8mb4_unicode_ci',
            'prefix' => '',
            'prefix_indexes' => true,
            'strict' => true,
            'engine' => null,
            'options' => extension_loaded('pdo_mysql') ? array_
            filter([
                PDO::MYSQL_ATTR_SSL_CA => env('MYSQL_ATTR_
                SSL_CA'),
            ]) : [],
    ],
```

The url, host, and port values are taken from the .env environment file. This is a good practice, rather than hard-coding the secret values in scm. To set the right values, open up .env file in the project root. You will find the following section:

```
DB_CONNECTION=mysql
DB_HOST=127.0.0.1
DB_PORT=3306
DB_DATABASE=laravel
DB_USERNAME=root
DB_PASSWORD=
```

Once updated, make sure to clear the cache and update the config cache with this change by running the following commands:

```
php artisan cache:clear
php artisan config:cache
```

The output is shown in Figure 14-3.

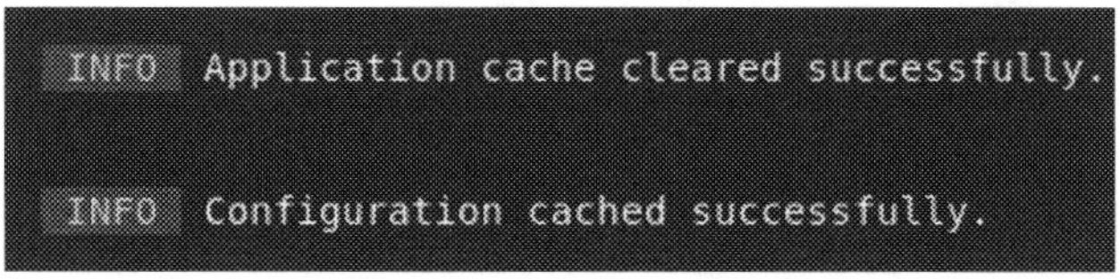

Figure 14-3. *Laravel cache cleaning command output*

Replace DB_DATABASE with your blog value and also set a DB_USERNAME and DB_PASSWORD relevant to your MySQL setup.

Database Migrations

Laravel provides a command to create migrations:

```
php artisan make:migration <identity_name_for_operation>
```

You will create a table called users to store user data. Run the following command to accomplish this:

```
php artisan make:migration create_users_table --create=users
--table=users
```

The output is shown in Figure 14-4.

Figure 14-4. *Laravel DB table creation*

The create and table options suggest creating a table in the database and the name of the table.

On running git status, you'll see a new file created at database/migrations/2022_07_31_095213_create_users_table.php. The name may be similar for you, except the prefix, which adds a timestamp value to it. This does not create the table yet in the database. Let's review the contents of this file.

2022_07_31_095213_create_users_table.php

```php
use Illuminate\Database\Migrations\Migration;
use Illuminate\Database\Schema\Blueprint;
use Illuminate\Support\Facades\Schema;

return new class extends Migration
{
    /**
     * Run the migrations.
     *
     * @return void
     */
    public function up()
    {
        Schema::create('users', function (Blueprint $table) {
            $table->id();
            $table->timestamps();
        });
    }

    /**
     * Reverse the migrations.
     *
     * @return void
     */
    public function down()
    {
        Schema::dropIfExists('users');
    }
};
```

From this default template, you can see two functions named up and down. up is used to execute the current change in a migration and down is used to revert the change. Inside the up function you can see the create call with two fields, id and timestamps. Let's execute the migration to see the change reflected in your database. Before running the following command, please make sure to remove any preexisting migration files that might have come with the initial setup in the database/migrations directory. Also, make sure your vendor/laravel/sanctum/database/migrations directory is empty too.

```
php artisan migrate
```

The output is shown in Figure 14-5.

Figure 14-5. *Laravel migrating output*

Refreshing your tables in phpMyAdmin shows two tables, as shown in Figure 14-6.

Figure 14-6. *Laravel table refreshing output*

The migrations table is a Laravel-specific table created to track the migration changes. Figure 14-7 shows a quick look at the migrations table schema, which specifies the one migration you did just now.

Figure 14-7. *List of tables*

Reviewing the users table schema shown in Figure 14-8, you see that it has a primary key id and two timestamp fields. You may need a few more fields like name, email, and password. You'll add them in following section.

#	Name	Type	Collation	Attributes	Null	Default	Comments	Extra	Action			
1	id 🔑	bigint(20)		UNSIGNED	No	None		AUTO_INCREMENT	✏ Change	⊘ Drop	More
2	created_at	timestamp			Yes	NULL			✏ Change	⊘ Drop	More
3	updated_at	timestamp			Yes	NULL			✏ Change	⊘ Drop	More

Figure 14-8. *Laravel table schema*

Create a new migration file as follows:

```
php artisan make:migration update_users_table --table=users
```

The output is shown in Figure 14-9.

```
INFO  Created migration [2022_07_31_143723_update_users_table].
```

Figure 14-9. *New migration file*

Open the new migration file in the database/migrations directory, which looks like the following:

```
<?php
```

```php
use Illuminate\Database\Migrations\Migration;
use Illuminate\Database\Schema\Blueprint;
use Illuminate\Support\Facades\Schema;

return new class extends Migration
{
    /**
     * Run the migrations.
     *
     * @return void
     */
    public function up()
    {
        Schema::table('users', function (Blueprint $table) {
            //
        });
    }

    /**
     * Reverse the migrations.
     *
     * @return void
     */
    public function down()
    {
        Schema::table('users', function (Blueprint $table) {
            //
        });
    }
};
```

Let's update the up method to contain the changes you want to bring in this migration and the down method with the reverse changes so as to remove them in case of a rollover:

```
/**
 * Run the migrations.
 *
 * @return void
 */
public function up()
{
    Schema::table('users', function (Blueprint $table) {
        $table->string('name');
        $table->string('email');
        $table->string('password');
    });
}

public function down()
{
    Schema::table('users', function (Blueprint $table) {
        $table->dropColumn('name');
        $table->dropColumn('email');
        $table->dropColumn('password');
    });
}
```

Now run the migrations:

```
php artisan migrate
```

The output is shown in Figure 14-10.

```
INFO  Running migrations.

2022_07_31_143723_update_users_table                               50.77ms DONE
```

Figure 14-10. *Laravel migrating output*

On revisiting the table schema, it has your changes. See Figure 14-11.

#	Name	Type	Collation	Attributes	Null	Default	Comments	Extra	Action		
1	id 🔑	bigint(20)		UNSIGNED	No	None		AUTO_INCREMENT	Change	Drop	More
2	created_at	timestamp			Yes	NULL			Change	Drop	More
3	updated_at	timestamp			Yes	NULL			Change	Drop	More
4	name	varchar(255)	utf8mb4_unicode_ci		No	None			Change	Drop	More
5	email	varchar(255)	utf8mb4_unicode_ci		No	None			Change	Drop	More
6	password	varchar(255)	utf8mb4_unicode_ci		No	None			Change	Drop	More

Figure 14-11. *Changes in the table schema*

Since the users table is set up, you can now create the user registration feature. There are three subfeatures of it functionality-wise that you will build:

1. Controller route to load the registration view form and accept form submit requests

2. Registration view form

3. Store user data in a database

Controller Route

When you visit http://localhost:8000/register, you get the page displayed in Figure 14-12, which is 404 not found, since you do not yet have a route for this URL in your controller.

Figure 14-12. *Laravel not-found page*

On opening routes/web.php you see the following content:

```php
<?php

use Illuminate\Support\Facades\Route;

/*
|----------------------------------------------------------------
------------
| Web Routes
|----------------------------------------------------------------
------------
|
| Here is where you can register web routes for your
    application. These
| routes are loaded by the RouteServiceProvider within a
    group which
```

```
| contains the "web" middleware group. Now create
  something great!
|
*/

Route::get('/', function () {
    return view('welcome');
});
```

Let's create a sample view page file in the resources/views/ directory named register.blade.php and set its content as follows to start with:

Registration Page

To load this page, add a route for the /register path as follows in routes/web.php file:

```
Route::get('/register', function () {
    return view('register');
});
```

Inspecting this code, it is evident that get specifies the REST API verb and /register the relative URI path for the get request. When the controller intercepts a get request to the /register path, it will return the register.blade.php page through a call to view('register').

Save the file and then visit http://localhost:8000/register and you should see the output shown in Figure 14-13.

Registration Page

Figure 14-13. Registration page

You will develop the registration form later. For now, let's create a sample view page for the registration success page and the other route for accepting the form submit request for registration submission.

The registration success page is at `resources/views/registration_success.blade.php`.

```
You have been successfully registered!
```

The following code should be added to `routes/web.php`:

```
Route::post('/register', function () {
    return view('registration_success');
});
```

The above route is for a post route request sent to the `/register` path and it returns the `registration_success` page. You will process the data later.

To test this change, either open a terminal with the `curl` command or Postman. Postman is a UI interface to run API requests. Further documentation related to its installation and usage can be found at `https://learning.postman.com/docs/getting-started/introduction/`.

curl request:

```
curl --location --request POST 'http://localhost:8000/register'
```

The output is shown in Figure 14-14.

```
ba(26,32,44,var(--bg-opacity)))).dark\:border-gray-700{--border-opacity:1;border-col
or:#4a5568;border-color:rgba(74,85,104,var(--border-opacity))}.dark\:text-white{--t
ext-opacity:1;color:#fff;color:rgba(255,255,255,var(--text-opacity))}.dark\:text-gr
ay-400{--text-opacity:1;color:#cbd5e0;color:rgba(203,213,224,var(--text-opacity))}}
        </style>

        <style>
            body {
                font-family: ui-sans-serif, system-ui, -apple-system, BlinkMacSyste
mFont, "Segoe UI", Roboto, "Helvetica Neue", Arial, "Noto Sans", sans-serif, "Apple
 Color Emoji", "Segoe UI Emoji", "Segoe UI Symbol", "Noto Color Emoji";
            }
        </style>
    </head>
    <body class="antialiased">
        <div class="relative flex items-top justify-center min-h-screen bg-gray-100
 dark:bg-gray-900 sm:items-center sm:pt-0">
            <div class="max-w-xl mx-auto sm:px-6 lg:px-8">
                <div class="flex items-center pt-8 sm:justify-start sm:pt-0">
                    <div class="px-4 text-lg text-gray-500 border-r border-gray-400
 tracking-wider">
                        419                            </div>

                    <div class="ml-4 text-lg text-gray-500 uppercase tracking-wider
">
                        Page Expired                            </div>
                </div>
            </div>
        </div>
    </body>
</html>
```

Figure 14-14. *curl request comment output*

The Postman request is shown in Figure 14-15.

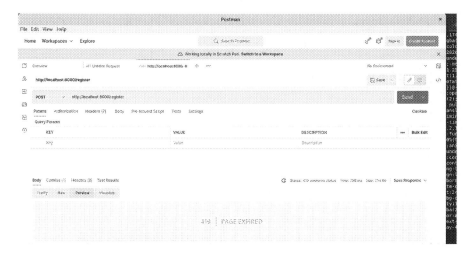

Figure 14-15. *Postman request output*

The output should load 419 | Page expired. This is a security mechanism which expects a csrf token. We will go into more details when you build the registration form. This output should verify that at least your POST route for the register works.

Registration View Form

Laravel's blade engine provides many built-in features to load, loop, parse data, and use in-built functions as needed. You will learn how to create a form that takes as input a few fields and submits them to your /register POST route.

To add form capabilities, install the following package, which has this feature, by running this command:

```
composer require laravelcollective/html
```

You make changes to the view file at resources/view/registration_success.blade.php by adding

Registration Page

```
{{ Form::open(array('url' => 'register')) }}
    // Form fields
{{ Form::close() }}
```

This creates a basic form HTML element with a form action URL set to the /register route and a csrf token for XSS protection, as you can see from the dev tools inspection in Figure 14-16.

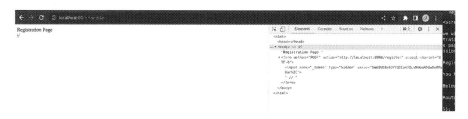

Figure 14-16. *Updated registration page*

Next, let's add a few fields that a user should fill in when registering.

1. Name field

```
{{ Form::label('name', 'Name'); }}
{{ Form::text('name'); }}
```

2. Email field

```
{{ Form::label('email', 'Email'); }}
{{ Form::email('email', $value = null, $attributes = array()); }}
```

3. Password field

```
{{ Form::label('password', 'Password'); }}
{{ Form::password('password'); }}
```

4. Submit button

```
{{ Form::submit('Register'); }}
```

These field elements should be added between the Form::open and Form::close calls.

The final view page code should like the following:

```
Registration Page
<br/>
<br/>
{{ Form::open(array('url' => 'register')) }}

{{ Form::label('name', 'Name'); }}
{{ Form::text('name'); }}
<br/>
<br/>
{{ Form::label('email', 'Email'); }}
{{ Form::email('email', $value = null, $attributes =
array()); }}
<br/>
<br/>
{{ Form::label('password', 'Password'); }}
{{ Form::password('password'); }}
<br/>
<br/>
{{ Form::submit('Register'); }}

{{ Form::close() }}
```

Reloading the page should show output like Figure 14-17.

Figure 14-17. *Refreshed registration page*

Try filling in the field details with some sample values and click the Register button to see the form POST submit request in action. On submitting, it will look like Figure 14-18.

You have been successfully registered!

Figure 14-18. *Successful registration page*

Storing User Data in a Database

You have the view and controllers set up, but you are not yet doing anything with the data. One of the important parts is to parse the POST request-submitted data, validate it, and then save it to the database. To keep it simple, you will only parse the data and save it to the database. Note that validation is very important before processing user-submitted data.

Now that you have been able to post data to a route end, you will parse the different values. These values are available as part of the Request object passed to the route method. Let's see it in practice. Make the following changes to the post route method in `routes/web.php`:

```
use Illuminate\Http\Request;

....
```

```
Route::post('/register', function (Request $request) {
    return view('registration_success');
});
```

Different values can be accessed by accessing properties on the $request object. For example, to fetch the email value, use $request-> email. Now you know how to parse the different post parameters, so you can proceed to using these values to save them in database.

Laravel uses Eloquent, which is an object relational mapper (ORM), which makes it very flexible to interact with databases. With this approach, each table has a respective model that is used to interact with that table.

```
Eloquent reference: https://laravel.com/docs/9.x/eloquent
ORM: https://en.wikipedia.org/wiki/
Object%E2%80%93relational_mapping
```

Let's create a model for your user table at app/Models/User.php with the following command:

```
php artisan make:model User
```

The output is shown in Figure 14-19.

INFO Model created successfully.

Figure 14-19. *Model creation output*

If you want to create a migration file at same time, please add the --migration option.

```
php artisan make:model User --migration
```

This creates a file at app/Models/User.php with the following default template:

```
<?php
```

```php
namespace App\Models;

use Illuminate\Database\Eloquent\Factories\HasFactory;
use Illuminate\Database\Eloquent\Model;

class User extends Model
{
    use HasFactory;
}
```

To add more fields, such as name, email, and password, add the following code to the class body:

```php
/**
 * The attributes that are mass assignable.
 *
 * @var array<int, string>
 */
protected $fillable = [
    'name',
    'email',
    'password',
];

/**
 * The attributes that should be hidden for serialization.
 *
 * @var array<int, string>
 */
protected $hidden = [
    'password',
];
```

Now your User model is ready to be used. To use the User model in your controller, update routes/web.php with the following namespace to declare the User model:

```
use App\Models\User;
```

....

```
Route::post('/register', function (Request $request) {
    User::create([
        'name' => $request->name,
        'email' => $request->email,
        'password' => Hash::make($request->password)
    ]);
    return view('registration_success');
});
```

This will save the user details in the user table and return the registration success template to the user. Notice you are using the Hash helper to one-way hash the password so that the password is stored in an encrypted format in database for security purpose. The output is shown in Figure 14-20.

Figure 14-20. *Updated registration output*

Let's also check the database for the user details stored with an encrypted password, as shown in Figure 14-21.

Figure 14-21. *Laravel DB encrypted password*

Summary

In this chapter, you went through the essential elements to get started with Laravel. You explored some of the main Laravel features but in general there are many more that you will find handy, along with a plethora of packages that are present in the Composer repository. Always check the documentation of Laravel to see if there is an existing component, helper, or library that can helps you with your task before checking the Composer libraries or creating a custom library. This will save you a lot of time in terms of development and maintenance. Laravel is continuously improving, so always follow Laravel news, email lists, and newsletters to stay up to date.

In the next chapter, you will focus on another PHP framework named Symfony, which is a very popular PHP framework already used by thousands of web applications.

CHAPTER 15

Introduction to Symfony

In the previous chapters, you learned how to use Lavarel, which is a web application framework used with PHP. In this chapter, you will focus on Symfony, which is a very popular PHP framework already used to develop websites and applications, including a very nice number of reusable PHP components.

This chapter consists of the following sections:

- Introduction to Symfony
- Installing Symfony
- Creating a Symfony Application

Introduction to Symfony

Symfony is a full-stack framework built using a standard set of reusable components. It's a project where you can choose to use some of its components or use the full stack.

It was created by Fabien Potencier in 2005 and is sponsored by SensioLabs. In Symfony's own words, *"Symfony is a set of PHP Components, a Web Application framework, a Philosophy, and a Community - all working together in harmony"* (`https://symfony.com/what-is-symfony`)

© Gunnard Engebreth, Satej Kumar Sahu 2023
G. Engebreth and S. K. Sahu, *PHP 8 Basics*, https://doi.org/10.1007/978-1-4842-8082-9_15

Breaking down and getting deeper into this summary:

A PHP framework:

A framework, as you know, is a foundational template to build upon. It consists of

1. A toolbox

   This is a set of reusable components in different contexts of security,* validation, processing, session handling, and more. These foundational elements make our job easier.

2. A process to do things

   There are frameworks that are flexible enough to have different structures, naming conventions, and control flow as per your wishes, and there are frameworks that have a conventional way of doing things. Symfony falls into the latter category. It requires some initial learning to understand these conventions but, once learned, they make our job easier in terms of using existing components, maintaining them, and easily creating similar structures through automated tools like command-line tools.

A philosophy:

Symfony was created from the imagination of web creators at SensioLabs. It was created *by* web creators *for* creators. These creators understand the needs of developers creating web applications. Symfony is created under an open source license, making it open to contributions, improvements, and reuse by the open community, thus bringing in ideas from the best minds.

A community:

Symfony is supported and contributed to *by* the community *for* the community. Symfony community support includes GitHub, Slack chat, and SesioLabs.

Features of Symfony: Symfony includes a number of key features that distinguish it from other frameworks. It's a very PHP-flexible framework, which is very important for a PHP web developer. It's easy to customize, including full-stack and brick-by-brick. Finally, it is very stable and sustainable.

1. PHP framework for web projects

    Symfony helps you quickly create and maintain PHP web applications. It also helps you avoid repetitive coding tasks and manage code controlling and versioning.

2. Ease of use

    Symfony is very easy to use because it is very flexible to any developer needs and is also very accessible. It comes with a lot of documentation and is supported by a strong community of professionals. It is also very easy to use for beginners because it includes embedded best practices.

3. Stable

    The release cadence of Symfony makes sure to maintain compatibility between minor versions of all releases and also provides three-year support for all major Symfony versions. This enables a stable and sustainable model that you can trust.

4. Extensible

    The integral central part of Symfony is made of reusable components that can be used in other projects or frameworks. This enables Symfony to be very flexible and also extensible with changes to the core behavior of the framework. Along with this, Symfony leverages Composer to integrate the ever-growing list of open source packages, thus enabling developers to easily enrich its ecosystem.

5. Fast

Fast is something everyone desires in terms of performance, but it is very hard to achieve. Symfony was built from the start to be fast with an emphasis on performance.

6. Dependency injection

Dependency injection is a core concept. It allows you to instantiate and use different components in the runtime. Symfony uses it to provide a centralized way for different objects to be initialized and provided in your application, thus enabling simplicity and modularity.

7. Modular elements

Symfony provides many out-of-the-box modular components for managing security, sessions, ORM features, forms, and a templating engine that can be included and fitted into use with Symfony with very little effort.

8. Profiler tool

The Profiler tool is part of every web page and is displayed at the bottom of all your pages. It provides profile information in a variety of contexts, which are discussed in coming sections. This is a very important tool in every developer's toolset. See Figure 15-1.

Figure 15-1. *Profiler toolset*

In Figure 15-1, you can see a toolbar with summary statistics. It's the development toolbar displayed by Symfony in debug mode and it contains many details for each unique page. Figure 15-2 shows the controller route, API response status, request time, memory usage, errors in form, and error logs.

Figure 15-2. *Profiler toolset components for status, time, memory usage, errors, and logs*

Other information includes

- Translation info
- Security info
- Twig/template calls
- Server info
- Symfony config info

Clicking on any one of them lets you further delve into the details. For example, Figure 15-3 shows that clicking on the request panel reveals further details related to the request.

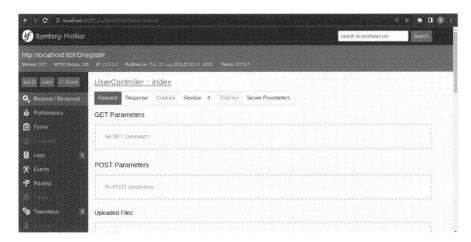

Figure 15-3. *Request panel*

On the left panel, you can also access further parts of the details related to the current page you are trying to access.

1. Command line tools

    The Symfony `cli` and `bin` commands allow you to create many starter templates like controllers, entity models, and migrations without doing a deep dive into them. In the following sections and coming chapter, you will see how helpful they are, thus making the development experience joyful.

2. Documentation and support

    The documentation of Symfony is unparalleled, with all small details from Getting Started guides, installation, and tutorials to API-specific documentations. The open community is always present to answer questions and provide support over the Stack Overflow platform and other forums. If you are more of a bookworm and want to read in detail, they have an online book (`https://symfony.com/book`) for your reference. They also provide Symfony training through certification coaching, the SensioLabs University eLearning platform, and video tutorials. Symfony also provides a certification, which is widely valued and is a feat to achieve.

Installing Symfony

There are a variety of ways by which Symfony can be installed. Refer to `https://symfony.com/doc/current/setup.html`.

You will be following the simplest one to get you up and running. Please make sure these prerequisites are installed before proceeding:

- PHP 8.1 or above

- PHP extensions: Ctype, iconv, PCRE, Session, SimpleXML, and Tokenizer. These extensions come installed by default with a PHP 8 installation.

- Composer tool to install Symfony and dependent packages

Before you create a basic Symfony project in the next chapter, let's install the Symfony CLI, which is very helpful in many tasks. Based on the operating system, there are different ways to install it; see `https://symfony.com/download`.

In a Ubuntu/Debian system, it can be run using the following commands:

```
curl -1sLf 'https://dl.cloudsmith.io/public/symfony/stable/
setup.deb.sh' | sudo -E bash
sudo apt install symfony-cli
```

The outcome of your Symfony installation is shown in Figure 15-4.

Figure 15-4. *Installation of Symfony*

Once the Symfony CLI is installed, you can use it to verify if your system meets all requirements for a Symfony application by running the following command:

```
symfony check:requirements
```

You should get an output similar to Figure 15-5 if all is good to proceed.

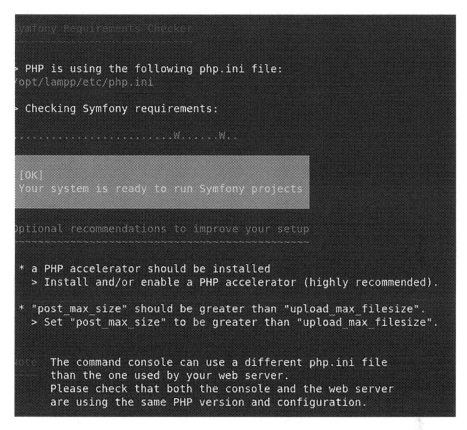

Figure 15-5. *Symfony installation verification*

Now that Symfony is installed, let's create your first application.

Creating a Symfony Application

To start a new project with the name of blog-app, run the following command:

```
composer create-project symfony/skeleton:"6.1.*" basic-
starter-app
cd basic-starter-app
composer require webapp
```

Anatomy of a Basic Symfony Application

Every installed Symfony application comes with a very basic directory structure with reusable components. The basic directory structure is shown in Figure 15-6.

```
app/
    The application configuration, templates and translations.

bin/
    Executable files (e.g. bin/console).

src/
    The project's PHP code.

tests/
    Automatic tests (e.g. Unit tests).

var/
    Generated files (cache, logs, etc.).

vendor/
    The third-party dependencies.

web/
    The web root directory.
```

Figure 15-6. *Symfony directory structure*

Figure 15-6 shows the responsibilities of the respective subdirectories with all the information. The basic Symfony application structure can be found at the Symfony official web page at https://symfony.com/doc/current/bundles/best_practices.html#directory-structure.

Once the project has been created, start it using the following commands:

```
cd basic-starter-app
symfony server:start
```

You can now access the app at `http://localhost:8000`, as shown in Figure 15-7.

Figure 15-7. *New app*

This should confirm a valid installation and setup of Symfony.

Summary

In this chapter, you learned about Symfony, a modern framework that can be used by you to build websites. It provides a flexible core and an ever-growing ecosystem of packages. You learned when to use this framework and how to use it.

In the next chapter, you will learn how to develop a basic Symfony application.

CHAPTER 16

A Basic Symfony Application

In the previous chapter, you installed and explored the Symfony PHP framework. In this chapter, you will focus on developing a basic Symfony application.

This chapter consists of the following sections.

- Creating a New Symfony Project
- Database Setup and Configuration
- Database Migrations
- Controller Route
- Registration View Form
- Storing User Data in a Database

Creating a New Symfony Project

Since you installed Symfony in the previous chapter, let's start by creating a new project with the name of blog-app and running the following command:

```
composer create-project symfony/skeleton:"6.1.*" blog-app
cd blog-app
composer require webapp
```

© Gunnard Engebreth, Satej Kumar Sahu 2023
G. Engebreth and S. K. Sahu, *PHP 8 Basics*, https://doi.org/10.1007/978-1-4842-8082-9_16

While installing the app-specific packages, it may ask if you need Docker-specific configuration settings that will enable you to run your Symfony application in a Dockerized environment. Please refer to the Symfony setup Docker installation web page for more information: `https://symfony.com/doc/current/setup/docker.html`.

Ignore it for now and say no. All information about the Symfony directory structure is provided in Chapter 15.

The Symfony CLI provides a very handy command to check the security of all the installed packages to ensure they are safe:

```
symfony check:security
```

The output showing if any Symfony package has any known vulnerabilities is shown in Figure 16-1.

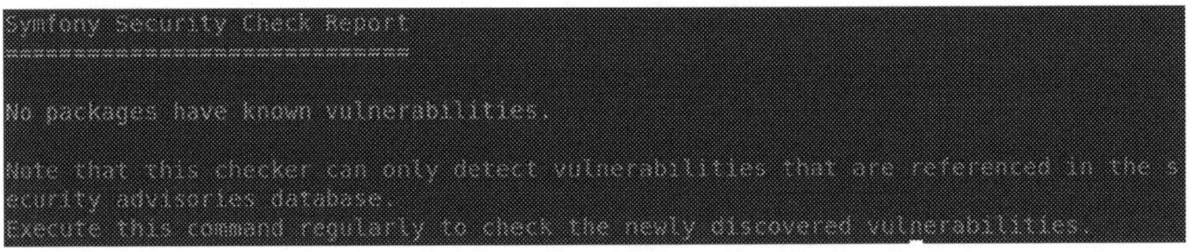

Figure 16-1. *No known vulnerabilities*

Once the project has been created, start it using the following commands:

```
cd blog-app
symfony server:start
```

The output of starting the Symfony web server is shown in Figure 16-2.

```
[WARNING] run "symfony server:ca:install" first if you want to run the web serve
r with TLS support, or use "--p12" or "--no-tls" to avoid this warning


Following Web Server log file (/home/vagrant/.symfony5/log/b3f26f9bfb27a239c124da3a
0493f2ac0d1eb88c.log)
Following PHP-CGI log file (/home/vagrant/.symfony5/log/b3f26f9bfb27a239c124da3a049
3f2ac0d1eb88c/79ca75f9e90b4126a5955a33ea6a41ec5e854698.log)

[WARNING] The local web server is optimized for local development and MUST never
 be used in a production setup.


[OK] Web server listening
     The Web server is using PHP CGI 8.1.6
     http://127.0.0.1:8000


[Web Server ] Aug  6 18:59:46 |DEBUG  | PHP    Reloading PHP versions
[Web Server ] Aug  6 18:59:46 |DEBUG  | PHP    Using PHP version 8.1.6 (from defaul
t version in $PATH)
[Application] Aug  6 20:58:05 |INFO   | DEPREC User Deprecated: The "Monolog\Logger
" class is considered final. It may change without further notice as of its next ma
jor version. You should not extend it from "Symfony\Bridge\Monolog\Logger".
[Web Server ] Aug  6 18:59:46 |INFO   | PHP    listening path="/opt/lampp/bin/php-c
gi-8.1.6" php="8.1.6" port=34505
```

Figure 16-2. *Symfony web server started*

You can now access the app at http://localhost:8000, as shown in Figure 16-3.

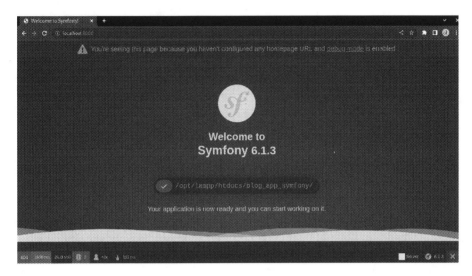

Figure 16-3. *Symfony dashboard web page*

This should confirm a valid installation and setup of Symfony. The development toolbar is shown in Figure 16-4.

Figure 16-4. *Symfony development toolbar*

The toolbar shows summary statistics. For more information, read Chapter 15.

Database Setup and Configuration

You will learn about various components of Symfony as you build one subpart of your blog application, which is user registration. Along the way, you will see how Symfony makes it easy for you to build such an application.

The core of any application is data, and you will need a database to store data related to your users.

You will create the table in an incremental fashion as you proceed through the different steps. In previous chapters, you created the database and tables manually using the phpMyAdmin interface. This usually works for a demo project, but while working on a production project it is usually suggested to maintain databases and tables in migrations, which are stored in files and can be committed to source code management systems like git.

This helps to have a repeatable data structure that can be readily used by other team members to get quickly onboarded and set up the project and also to create different environments for running a project like dev, staging, and production. This has the added benefit of a versioned schema of your database and tables to understand and maintain the history of changes for auditing and other such purposes.

Before you start setting up the migration aspect of Symfony, you need to configure the database configuration. The first step is to install the Doctrine orm package, which is a set of PHP libraries mainly focused on providing persistence services and functionalities.

```
$ composer require symfony/orm-pack
```

The output of the installation of Doctrine is shown in Figure 16-5.

```
Using version ^2.2 for symfony/orm-pack
./composer.json has been updated
Running composer update symfony/orm-pack
Loading composer repositories with package information
Updating dependencies
Lock file operations: 1 install, 0 updates, 0 removals
  - Locking symfony/orm-pack (v2.2.0)
Writing lock file
Installing dependencies from lock file (including require-dev)
Package operations: 1 install, 0 updates, 0 removals
  - Installing symfony/orm-pack (v2.2.0): Extracting archive
Generating optimized autoload files
109 packages you are using are looking for funding.
Use the `composer fund` command to find out more!

Run composer recipes at any time to see the status of your Symfony recipes.

Unpacking Symfony packs
  - Unpacked symfony/orm-pack
Loading composer repositories with package information
Updating dependencies
Nothing to modify in lock file
Installing dependencies from lock file (including require-dev)
Package operations: 0 installs, 0 updates, 1 removal
  - Removing symfony/orm-pack (v2.2.0)
Generating optimized autoload files
108 packages you are using are looking for funding.
Use the `composer fund` command to find out more!

Run composer recipes at any time to see the status of your Symfony recipes.

Executing script cache:clear[Application] Aug 21 10:42:46 |INFO   | DEPREC User Dep
recated: The "Monolog\Logger" class is considered final. It may change without furt
her notice as of its next major version. You should not extend it from "Symfony\Bri
dge\Monolog\Logger".
 [OK]
Executing script assets:install public [OK]

No security vulnerability advisories found

No security vulnerability advisories found
```

Figure 16-5. *Installation of the Doctrine package*

Let's install and enable this bundle in your application, as shown in Figure 16-6.

```
$ composer require --dev symfony/maker-bundle
```

```
Using version ^1.45 for symfony/maker-bundle
./composer.json has been updated
Running composer update symfony/maker-bundle
Loading composer repositories with package information
Updating dependencies
Nothing to modify in lock file
Writing lock file
Installing dependencies from lock file (including require-dev)
Nothing to install, update or remove
Generating optimized autoload files
108 packages you are using are looking for funding.
Use the `composer fund` command to find out more!

Run composer recipes at any time to see the status of your Symfony recipes.

Executing script cache:clear
 [OK]
Executing script assets:install public [OK]

No security vulnerability advisories found
```

Figure 16-6. *Install and enable this bundle in your application*

Now update the database-relevant values inside the .env file. Comment out the PostgreSQL URL and uncomment the MySQL URL line above it. Then update

```
DATABASE_URL="mysql://app:!ChangeMe!@127.0.0.1:3306/app?serverV
ersion=8&charset=utf8mb4"
```

with

```
DATABASE_URL="mysql://root:password@127.0.0.1:3306/blog"
```

Now let's create the database by running the following command:

```
$ php bin/console doctrine:database:create
```

The output of the database creation is shown in Figure 16-7.

```
$ php bin/console doctrine:database:create
Created database `blog` for connection named default
$
```

Figure 16-7. *Database creation*

You can review phpMyAdmin to confirm it. See Figure 16-8.

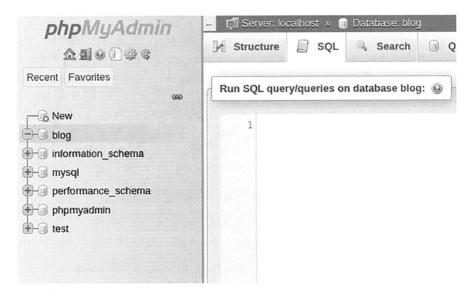

Figure 16-8. *phpMyAdmin tool to review and confirm changes*

You will need an entity to represent your user object. Let's create it by running the following command:

```
$ php bin/console make:entity
```

This will ask the name of the entity, which in your case is User, and any fields and their types to be defined.

The output of this command is shown in Figure 16-9.

```
$ php bin/console make:entity

Class name of the entity to create or update (e.g. VictoriousKangaroo):
> User

 created: src/Entity/User.php
 created: src/Repository/UserRepository.php

Entity generated! Now let's add some fields!
You can always add more fields later manually or by re-running this command.

New property name (press <return> to stop adding fields):
> name

Field type (enter ? to see all types) [string]:
> string

Field length [255]:
>

Can this field be null in the database (nullable) (yes/no) [no]:
> no

updated: src/Entity/User.php

Add another property? Enter the property name (or press <return> to stop adding fi
elds):
> █
```

Figure 16-9. *Create User entity*

Similarly, also add fields for email and password. Once done, simply
enter without entering any value. After making these changes, you'll get a
success message, as shown in Figure 16-10.

```
updated: src/Entity/User.php

Add another property? Enter the property name (or press <return> to stop adding fi
elds):
>

 Success!

Next: When you're ready, create a migration with php bin/console make:migration
```

Figure 16-10. *User entity successfully created*

Let's verify the contents of the created file at src/Entity/User.php:

```php
<?php

namespace App\Entity;

use App\Repository\UserRepository;
use Doctrine\ORM\Mapping as ORM;

#[ORM\Entity(repositoryClass: UserRepository::class)]
class User
{
    #[ORM\Id]
    #[ORM\GeneratedValue]
    #[ORM\Column]
    private ?int $id = null;

    #[ORM\Column(length: 255)]
    private ?string $name = null;

    #[ORM\Column(length: 255)]
    private ?string $email = null;

    #[ORM\Column(length: 255)]
    private ?string $password = null;

    public function getId(): ?int
    {
        return $this->id;
    }

    public function getName(): ?string
    {
        return $this->name;
    }

    public function setName(string $name): self
```

```
{
    $this->name = $name;

    return $this;
}
public function getEmail(): ?string
{
    return $this->email;
}
public function setEmail(string $email): self
{
    $this->email = $email;

    return $this;
}
public function getPassword(): ?string
{
    return $this->password;
}
public function setPassword(string $password): self
{
    $this->password = $password;

    return $this;
}
}
```

You've added all the defined columns into attributes for the User
attributes. Using this you can now create your migration to create the table
in the database. Run the following:

```
php bin/console make:migration
```

The output of this command is shown in Figure 16-11.

Figure 16-11. *Migration successfully created*

Let's review the migration file created (in our case, it's at `migrations/`
`Version20220821091914.php`):

```php
<?php

declare(strict_types=1);

namespace DoctrineMigrations;

use Doctrine\DBAL\Schema\Schema;
use Doctrine\Migrations\AbstractMigration;

/**
 * Auto-generated Migration: Please modify to your needs!
 */
final class Version20220821091914 extends AbstractMigration
{
    public function getDescription(): string
    {
        return '';
    }

    public function up(Schema $schema): void
    {
```

```
    // this up() migration is auto-generated, please modify
    it to your needs
    $this->addSql('CREATE TABLE user (id INT AUTO_
    INCREMENT NOT NULL, name VARCHAR(255) NOT NULL, email
    VARCHAR(255) NOT NULL, password VARCHAR(255) NOT NULL,
    PRIMARY KEY(id)) DEFAULT CHARACTER SET utf8mb4 COLLATE
    `utf8mb4_unicode_ci` ENGINE = InnoDB');
    $this->addSql('CREATE TABLE messenger_messages (id
    BIGINT AUTO_INCREMENT NOT NULL, body LONGTEXT NOT NULL,
    headers LONGTEXT NOT NULL, queue_name VARCHAR(190)
    NOT NULL, created_at DATETIME NOT NULL, available_at
    DATETIME NOT NULL, delivered_at DATETIME DEFAULT
    NULL, INDEX IDX_75EA56E0FB7336F0 (queue_name),
    INDEX IDX_75EA56E0E3BD61CE (available_at), INDEX
    IDX_75EA56E016BA31DB (delivered_at), PRIMARY KEY(id))
    DEFAULT CHARACTER SET utf8mb4 COLLATE `utf8mb4_unicode_
    ci` ENGINE = InnoDB');
}

public function down(Schema $schema): void
{
    // this down() migration is auto-generated, please
    modify it to your needs
    $this->addSql('DROP TABLE user');
    $this->addSql('DROP TABLE messenger_messages');
}
}
```

The file has up and down methods for migrate and rollback. It contains your create table SQL. This is very handy as you do not need to create the SQL statement yourself. Run this migration:

```
php bin/console doctrine:migrations:migrate
```

The output of this command is shown in Figure 16-12.

```
$ php bin/console doctrine:migrations:migrate

WARNING! You are about to execute a migration in database "blog" that could result
in schema changes and data loss. Are you sure you wish to continue? (yes/no) [yes]
:
```

Figure 16-12. *Database migration*

Enter to proceed, as shown in Figure 16-13.

```
[notice] Migrating up to DoctrineMigrations\Version20220821091914
[notice] finished in 342.1ms, used 20M memory, 1 migrations executed, 2 sql queries
```

Figure 16-13. *Database migration completed*

Let's check phpMyAdmin to review the creation of the user and the migrations table, as shown in Figures 16-14 and 16-15.

Table ▲	Action							Rows	Type	Collation	Size	Overhead
☐ doctrine_migration_versions	☆	▥ Browse	⚡ Structure	⚲ Search	⧉ Insert	▦ Empty	⊘ Drop	1	InnoDB	utf8_unicode_ci	16.0 KiB	-
☐ messenger_messages	☆	▥ Browse	⚡ Structure	⚲ Search	⧉ Insert	▦ Empty	⊘ Drop	0	InnoDB	utf8mb4_unicode_ci	64.0 KiB	-
☐ user	☆	▥ Browse	⚡ Structure	⚲ Search	⧉ Insert	▦ Empty	⊘ Drop	0	InnoDB	utf8mb4_unicode_ci	16.0 KiB	-
3 tables	Sum							1	InnoDB	utf8mb4_general_ci	96.0 KiB	0 B
↑ ☐ Check all	With selected: ⌄											

Figure 16-14. *phpMyAdmin tool to see the user migrations table*

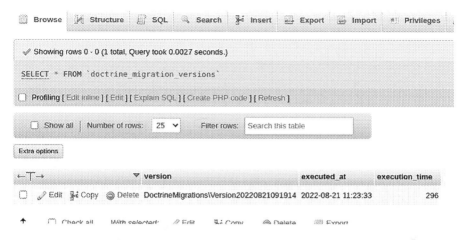

Figure 16-15. *phpMyAdmin tool to review creation*

The doctrine_migration_versions table is an internal Symfony-specific table created to track the migration changes. Figure 16-16 shows a quick look at the migrations table schema, which specifies the one migration you did just now.

#	Name	Type	Collation	Attributes	Null	Default	Comments	Extra	Action		
1	id	int(11)			No	None		AUTO_INCREMENT	Change	Drop	More
2	name	varchar(255)	utf8mb4_unicode_ci		No	None			Change	Drop	More
3	email	varchar(255)	utf8mb4_unicode_ci		No	None			Change	Drop	More
4	password	varchar(255)	utf8mb4_unicode_ci		No	None			Change	Drop	More

Figure 16-16. *Migration table schema*

With these changes, if you now start the Symfony server, you will see a few logs related to connecting to the database and executing some system-level queries.

Now, since the user table is set up, you can create the user registration feature. There are three subfeatures of it functionality-wise that you will build:

1. Controller route to load the registration view form and accept form submit requests

2. Registration view form

3. Storing user data in a database

Controller Route

Let's see now how to work with the Controller Route to load the registration view form and accept form submit requests.

When you visit the `http://localhost:8000/register` URL, you get the page shown in Figure 16-17, a 404 not found code, since you do not have a route for this URL in your controller.

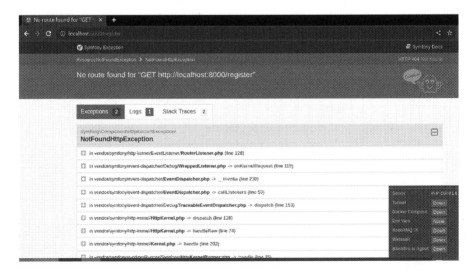

Figure 16-17. *Register web page*

If you see a "The metadata storage is not up to date, please run the sync-metadata-storage command to fix this issue" message, please run the following command to fix it:

```
$ php bin/console doctrine:migrations:sync-metadata-storage
```

Let's create a controller to handle this route.

```
$ php bin/console make:controller UserController
```

The output of this command is shown in Figure 16-18.

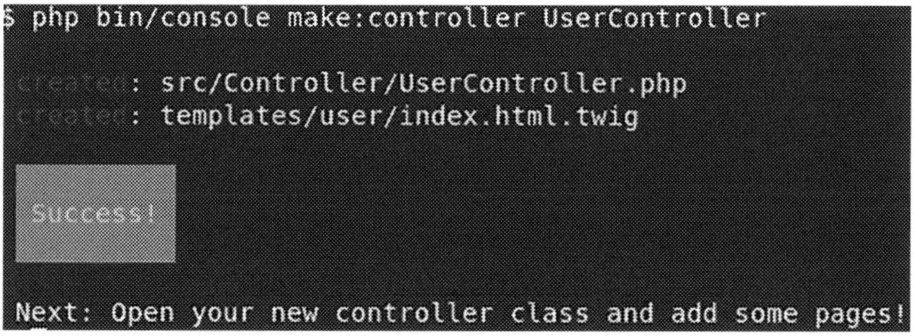

Figure 16-18. *UserController created*

It created two files at

```
src/Controller/UserController.php
templates/user/index.html.twig
```

Let's review the contents of src/Controller/UserController.php.

```php
<?php

namespace App\Controller;

use Symfony\Bundle\FrameworkBundle\Controller\
AbstractController;
use Symfony\Component\HttpFoundation\Response;
```

```php
use Symfony\Component\Routing\Annotation\Route;

class UserController extends AbstractController
{
    #[Route('/user', name: 'app_user')]
    public function index(): Response
    {
        return $this->render('user/index.html.twig', [
            'controller_name' => 'UserController',
        ]);
    }
}
```

Let's modify the route from /user to /register and reload your browser at http://localhost:8000/register.

```php
class UserController extends AbstractController
{
    #[Route('/register', name: 'app_user')]
```

The output of the code is shown in Figure 16-19.

Figure 16-19. UserController code output

Inspecting the above code, if no GET or POST method is mentioned, by default it's a GET request and /register is the relative URI path for the GET request. When the controller intercepts a GET request to the /register path, it will return the user/index.html.twig page through a call to the render function.

You will develop the registration form later. For now, let's create a sample view page for registration success page and another route for accepting the form submit request for registration submission.

See the registration success page at `templates/user/registration_success.html.twig`. You have been successfully registered!

Update the GET route with the following code at `src/Controller/UserController.php` to add a POST request handler:

```
....

use Symfony\Component\HttpFoundation\Request;

....

    #[Route('/register', name: 'app_user', methods: ['GET',
    'POST'])]
    public function index(Request $request): Response
    {
        if ($request->isMethod('POST')) {
            return $this->render('user/registration_success.
            html.twig', [
                'controller_name' => 'UserController',
            ]);
        }
        ...

        // Previous code for GET response
    }
```

The above route now handles both GET and POST requests for the /register route, and when a POST request is sent to the /register path, it returns the registration_success page. You have left out the processing of data and will complete it later.

To test this change, either open a terminal with a `curl` command or use Postman. Postman is a UI interface to run API requests. Further documentation related to installation and usage can be found at `https://learning.postman.com/docs/getting-started/introduction/`.

The `curl` request command is the following:

```
curl --location --request POST 'http://localhost:8000/register'
```

The output of this command is shown in Figure 16-20.

```
$ curl --location --request POST 'http://localhost:8000/register'
You have been successfully registered!
```

Figure 16-20. *Register command output*

The Postman request is shown in Figure 16-21.

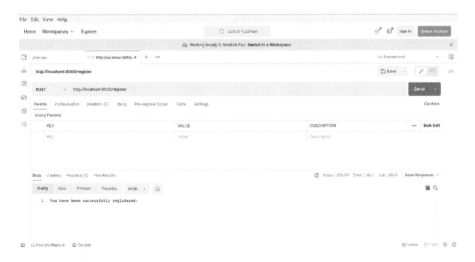

Figure 16-21. *Register command output in the Postman tool*

Registration View Form

Symfony's twig template engine provides many built-in features to load, loop, parse data, and use built-in functions as needed. You will learn how to create a form that takes as input a few fields and submits them to your /register POST route.

To add form capabilities, install the following package, which has this feature, by running this command:

```
composer require symfony/form
```

Symfony allows you to initiate a form through a FormBuilder method and associates the fields with the entity without you having to manage a lot of validations explicitly.

The first change is to create an instance of your User entity inside the index method.

```
...

use App\Entity\User;

...

    public function register(Request $request, ManagerRegistry
    $doctrine): Response
    {
        $user = new User();
        ...
```

You will now build the form using the form builder method and bind it to the $user instance.

```
        $form = $this->createFormBuilder($user)
        // Bind $user to the $form instance
        // Associate entity name field to $form and show it as
        a text type field
```

```
->add('name', TextType::class)
// Associate entity email field to $form and show as an
email type field
->add('email', TextType::class)
// Associate entity password field to $form and show as
a password type field
->add('password', PasswordType::class)
// Finally add a submit button
->add('save', SubmitType::class, ['label' =>
'Register'])
->getForm();
```

Once the form builder instance is created, you need to associate and pass $form onto the view layer, which is user/index.html.twig. This is done by updating the index render call with the following:

```
return $this->renderForm('user/index.html.twig', [
    'form' => $form,
]);
```

Start making changes to the view file at user/index.html.twig by replacing all content with the following code to use the created form:

```
{% extends 'base.html.twig' %}

{% block title %}Registration Page!{% endblock %}

{% block body %}
  {{ form(form) }}
{% endblock %}
```

In this code, you have replaced the title and block body with a simple call to form(form), which loads the passed-in form. This creates a basic form HTML element with three fields and a csrf token for XSS protection, as can be seen from the dev tools inspection shown in Figure 16-22.

Figure 16-22. *Basic registration view form example*

The final controller code should look as follows:

```php
<?php

namespace App\Controller;

use Symfony\Bundle\FrameworkBundle\Controller\
AbstractController;
use Symfony\Component\HttpFoundation\Request;
use Symfony\Component\HttpFoundation\Response;
use Symfony\Component\Routing\Annotation\Route;
use App\Entity\User;
use Symfony\Component\Form\Extension\Core\Type\TextType;
use Symfony\Component\Form\Extension\Core\Type\EmailType;
use Symfony\Component\Form\Extension\Core\Type\PasswordType;
use Symfony\Component\Form\Extension\Core\Type\SubmitType;

class UserController extends AbstractController
{
    #[Route('/register', name: 'app_user', methods: ['GET',
    'POST'])]
    public function index(Request $request): Response
    {
        $user = new User();
        $form = $this->createFormBuilder($user)
            ->add('name', TextType::class)
```

```
        ->add('email', EmailType::class)
        ->add('password', PasswordType::class)
        ->add('save', SubmitType::class, ['label' =>
        'Register'])
        ->getForm();

    if ($request->isMethod('POST')) {
        return $this->render('user/registration_success.
        html.twig', [
            'controller_name' => 'UserController',
        ]);
    }

    return $this->renderForm('user/index.html.twig', [
        'form' => $form,
    ]);
    }
}
```

Try filling in the field details with some sample value and click the Register button to see the form's POST submit request in action.

On submitting, it will display the output shown in Figure 16-23.

You have been successfully registered!

Figure 16-23. *Basic registration view form web page output*

Storing User Data in a Database

You have the view and controllers set up, but you are not doing anything with the data. One of the important parts is to parse the POST request-submitted data, validate it, and then save it to a database.

Now that you have been able to post data to a route end, you can parse the different values. These values are available as part of the Request object and can be used to associate with the form entity. Let's see it in practice. Make the following changes to the index method after $form is instantiated:

...

```
$form->handleRequest($request);
```

...

Now with above change, $form, which has been associated with your User entity, has the submitted values filled into the respective fields and can be used to fetch the User entity set to these values.

```
$user = $form->getData();
```

Before you fetch the form data, you need to validate if all is well and also you need to replace the isMethod function call check with a handy method which the form provides to check if it was submitted to give you an idea that this is a POST request:

```
if ($form->isSubmitted() && $form->isValid()) {
$user = $form->getData();
```

Now save the data to a database through Doctrine EntityManager. Before saving it, you need to encrypt your password for security purposes. Add the namespaces for ManagerRegistry and UserPasswordHasherInterface and pass them as an argument to index, so that Symfony through dependency injection can instantiate them and pass them to the function.

```
use Doctrine\Persistence\ManagerRegistry;
use Symfony\Component\PasswordHasher\Hasher\
UserPasswordHasherInterface;

...

    public function index(
        Request $request,
        ManagerRegistry $doctrine,
        UserPasswordHasherInterface $passwordHasher,
    ): Response
    {
        ...

            $user->setPassword(
                $passwordHasher->hashPassword($user, $user-
                >getPassword())
            );

            $entityManager = $doctrine->getManager();
            $entityManager->persist($user);
            $entityManager->flush();
```

This will save the user details in the user table and return the
registration success template to the user. Notice you are using Hash helper
to one-way hash the password so that the password is stored in encrypted
format in the database for security purposes.

The whole code should now look like the following:

```
<?php

namespace App\Controller;

use Symfony\Bundle\FrameworkBundle\Controller\
AbstractController;
use Symfony\Component\HttpFoundation\Request;
```

```
use Symfony\Component\HttpFoundation\Response;
use Symfony\Component\Routing\Annotation\Route;
use App\Entity\User;
use Symfony\Component\PasswordHasher\Hasher\
UserPasswordHasherInterface;
use Doctrine\Persistence\ManagerRegistry;
use Symfony\Component\Form\Extension\Core\Type\TextType;
use Symfony\Component\Form\Extension\Core\Type\EmailType;
use Symfony\Component\Form\Extension\Core\Type\PasswordType;
use Symfony\Component\Form\Extension\Core\Type\SubmitType;

class UserController extends AbstractController
{
    #[Route('/register', name: 'app_user', methods: ['GET',
    'POST'])]
    public function index (
        Request $request,
        ManagerRegistry $doctrine,
        UserPasswordHasherInterface $passwordHasher
    ): Response
    {
        $user = new User();
        $form = $this->createFormBuilder($user)
            ->add('name', TextType::class)
            ->add('email', EmailType::class)
            ->add('password', PasswordType::class)
            ->add('save', SubmitType::class, ['label' =>
            'Register'])
            ->getForm();

        $form->handleRequest($request);
```

```
if ($form->isSubmitted() && $form->isValid()) {
    $user = $form->getData();
    $user->setPassword($passwordHasher-
>hashPassword($user, $user->getPassword()));
    $entityManager = $doctrine->getManager();
    $entityManager->persist($user);
    $entityManager->flush();

    return $this->render('user/registration_success.
    html.twig', [
        'controller_name' => 'UserController',
    ]);
}

return $this->renderForm('user/index.html.twig', [
    'form' => $form,
]);
    }
}
```

Let's also check the database to see the user details stored with an encrypted password, as shown in Figure 16-24.

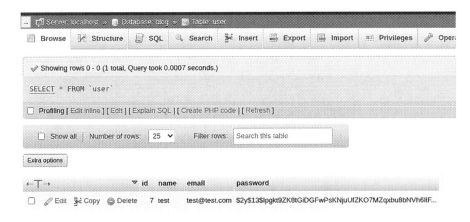

Figure 16-24. *Checking the database with an encrypted password*

Summary

In this chapter, you went through the essential elements to start with Symfony. You set up and configured a database and added data to it. You also learned about some of major features of Symfony. However, there are many more that you will find handy, along with a plethora of packages in the Composer repository.

This is the last chapter of this book. You've learned the basics of PHP version 8!

Index

A

Abstract classes, 33, 34, 39–41, 48

ACTUAL single quote, 53

API-specific documentations, 278

Application programming interface
(API), 26, 29, 30, 229, 235,
237, 239, 261, 276, 278, 304

app/Models/User.php, 268

Arbitrary cookie, 163

array_change_key_case(), 93

array_chunk(), 93, 94

array_column(), 94, 95

array_combine(), 95

array_count_values(), 95

array_diff(), 98, 99

array_diff_assoc(), 96

array_diff_key(), 96

array_diff_uassoc(), 97

array_diff_ukey(), 97, 98

array_fill(), 99, 100

array_fill_keys(), 99

array_filter(), 100, 101

ARRAY_FILTER_USE_BOTH, 100

ARRAY_FILTER_USE_KEY, 100

array_flip(), 101

Array functions
array(), 128, 129
array_change_key_case(), 93

array_chunk(), 93, 94

array_column(), 94, 95

array_combine(), 95

array_count_values(), 95

array_diff(), 98, 99

array_diff_assoc(), 96

array_diff_key(), 96

array_diff_uassoc(), 97

array_diff_ukey(), 97, 98

array_fill(), 99, 100

array_fill_keys(), 99

array_filter(), 100, 101

array_flip(), 101

array_intersect(), 104

array_intersect_assoc(), 101, 102

array_intersect_key(), 102

array_intersect_uassoc(), 102, 103

array_intersect_ukey(), 103, 104

array_is_list(), 104, 105

array_key(), 137

array_key_exists(), 105, 137

array_key_first(), 105

array_key_last(), 106

array_keys(), 106

array_map(), 107

array_merge(), 108, 109

array_merge_recursive(), 108

array_multisort(), 109

T

Printed in the United States
by Baker & Taylor Publisher Services